THE PROTOCOLS

OF THE MEETINGS OF THE LEARNED ELDERS OF ZION

THE PROTOCOLS

OF THE MEETINGS OF THE LEARNED ELDERS OF ZION

TRANSLATED BY VICTOR E. MARSDEN

(Antisemitic Forgery and Hoax)

ISBN: 978-93-5128-541-0

First Published in 1923
Indian Reprint in 2018

Published by

Kalpaz Publications
C-30, Satyawati Nagar,
Delhi – 110052
E-mail: kalpaz@hotmail.com
Website: kalpazpublications.com
Ph.: +91-9212142040

Cataloging in Publication Data—DK
Courtesy: D.K. Agencies (P) Ltd. <docinfo@dkagencies.com>

Protocols of the wise men of Zion. English.
The protocols of the meetings of the learned elders of zion / translated by Victor E. Marsden.
pages cm
Translated from Russian.
Translation of: Protocols of the wise men of Zion.
"First published in 1923"—Title page verso.
ISBN 9789351285410

1. Antisemitism. I. Marsden, Victor E. (Victor Emile), 1866-1920, translator. II. Title.

DS145.P5E5 2017 DDC 305.8924 23

PREFACE

(Translated by Victor E. Marsden)

The author of this translation of the famous Protocols was himself a victim of the Revolution. He had lived for many years in Russia and was married to a Russian lady. Among his other activities in Russia he had been for a number of years a Russian Correspondent of the MORNING POST, a position which he occupied when the Revolution broke out, and his vivid descriptions of events in Russia will still be in the recollection of many of the readers of that Journal. Naturally he was singled out for the anger of the Soviet. On the day that Captain Cromie was murdered by Jews, Victor Marsden was arrested and thrown into the Peter-Paul Prison, expecting every day to have his name called out for execution. This, however, he escaped, and eventually he was allowed to return to England very much of a wreck in bodily health. However, he recovered under treatment and the devoted care of his wife and friends. One of the first things he undertook, as soon as he was able, was this translation of the *Protocols*. Mr. Marsden was eminently well qualified for the work. His intimate acquaintance with Russia, Russian life and the Russian language on the one hand, and his mastery of a terse literary English style on the other, placed him in a position of advantage which few others could claim. The consequence is that we have in his version an eminently readable work, and though the subject-matter is somewhat formless, Mr. Marsden's literary touch reveals the thread running through the twenty-four *Protocols*. The summary placed at the head of each is Mr Marsden's own, and will be found very useful in acquiring a comprehensive view of its scope.

It may be said with truth that this work was carried out at the cost of Mr. Marsden's own life's blood. He told the writer of this *Preface* that he could not stand more than an hour at a time of his work on it in the British Museum, as the diabolical spirit of the matter which he was obliged to turn into English made him positively ill.

Mr. Marsden's connection with the *Morning Post* was not severed by his return to England, and he was well enough to accept the post of special correspondent of that journal in the suite of H.R.H., the Prince of Wales on his Empire tour. From this he returned with the Prince, apparently in much better health, but within a few days of his landing he was taken suddenly ill, and died after a very brief illness.

May this work be his crowning monument! In it he has performed an immense service to the English-speaking world, and there can be little doubt that it will take its place in the first rank of the English versions of *"THE PROTOCOLS of the Meetings of the* LEARNED ELDERS OF ZION."

INTRODUCTION

Of the Protocols themselves little need be said in the way of introduction. The book in which they are embodied was published by Sergyei Nilus in Russia in 1905. A copy of this is in the British Museum bearing the dated of its reception August 10, 1906. All copies that were known to exist in Russia were destroyed in the Kerensky regime, and under his successors the possession of a copy by anyone in Sovietland was a crime sufficient to ensure the owner's being shot on sight. The fact it in itself sufficient proof of the genuineness of the Protocols. The Jewish journals, of course, say that they are a forgery, leaving it to be understood that Professor Nilus, who embodied them in a work of his own, had concocted them for his own purposes.

M. Henry Ford, in an interview published in the New York World, February 17, 1921, put the case for Nilus tersely and convincingly thus:

> The only statement I care to make about the PROTOCOLS is that they fit in with what is going on. They are sixteen years old, and they have fitted the world situation up to this time. THEY FIT IT NOW.

Indeed they do!

The word "Protocol" signifies a precise gummed on to the front of a document, a draft of a document, minutes of proceedings. In this instance "Protocol" means "minutes of the proceedings" of the Meetings of the Learned Elders of Zion. These Protocols give the substance of addresses delivered to the innermost circle of the Rulers of Zion. They reveal the concerted plan of action of the Jewish Nation developed through the ages and edited by the Elders themselves up to date. Parts and summaries of the plan have been published from time to time during the centuries as the secrets of the Elders have leaked out. The claim of the Jews that the Protocols are forgeries is in itself an admission of their genuineness, for they *never attempt to answer that facts* corresponding to the *threats* which the Protocols contain, and, indeed, the correspondence between the prophecy and fulfillment is to glaring to be set aside or obscured. This the Jews well know and therefore evade.

The presumption is strong that the PROTOCOLS were issued, or reissued, at the First Zionist Congress held at Basel in 1897 under the presidency of the Father of Modern Zionism, the late Theodor Herzl.

There has been recently published a volume of Herzl's "Diaries," a translation of some passages of which appeared in the *Jewish Chronicle* of July 14, 1922. Herzl gives an account of his first visit to England in 1895, and his conversation with Colonel Goldsmid, a Jew brought up as a Christian, an Officer in the English Army, and at heart a Jew Nationalist all the time. goldsmid suggested to herzl that the best way of expropriating the English Aristocracy and so destroying their power to protect the people of England against Jew domination, was to put excessive taxes on the land. Herzl thought this an excellent idea, and it is now to be found definitely embodied in Protocol VI!

The above extract from Herzl's *Diary* is an extremely significant bit of evidence bearing on the existence of the Jew World Plot and authenticity of the Protocols, but any reader of intelligence will be able from his own knowledge of recent history and from his own experience to confirm the genuineness of every line of them, and it is in the light of this *living* comment that all readers are invited to study Mr. Marsden's translation of this terrible inhuman document.

And here is another very significant circumstance. The present successor of Herzl as leader of the Zionist movement, Dr. Weizmann, quoted one of these sayings at the send-off banquet given to Chief Rabbi Hertz on October 6, 1920. The Chief Rabbi was on the point of leaving for his Empire tour - a sort of Jewish answer to the Empire tour of H.R.H. the Prince of Wales. And this is the "saying" of the Sages which Dr. Weizmann quoted: "A beneficent protection which God has instituted in the life of the Jew is that He has dispersed him all over the world." (*Jewish Guardian,* Cot. 8, 1920.)

Now compare this with the last clause but one of Protocol XI,

"God has granted to us, His Chosen People, the gift of dispersion, and from this, which appears to all eyes to be our weakness, has come forth all strength, which has now brought us to the threshold of sovereignty over all the world."

The remarkable correspondence between these passages proves several things. It proves that the Learned Elders exist. It proves that Dr. Weizmann knows all about them. It proves that the desire for a "National Home" in Palestine is only camouflage and an infinitesimal part of the Jew's real object. It proves that the Jews of the world have no intentions of settling in Palestine or any separate country, and their annual prayer that they may all meet "Next Year in Jerusalem" is merely a piece of their characteristic make-believe. It also demonstrates that the Jews are now a world menace, and that the Aryan races will have to domicile them permanently out of Europe.

Who are the Elders?

This is a secret which has not been revealed. The are the Hidden Hand. They are not the "Board of Deputies" (the Jewish Parliament in England) or the "Universal Israelite Alliance" which sit in Paris. But the late Walter Rathenau of the Allgemeiner Electrizitaets Gesellschaft has thrown a little light on the subject and doubtless he was in possession of their names, being, in all likelihood, one of the chief leaders himself. Writing in the *Wiener Freie Presse,* December 24, 1912, he said:

> Three hundred men, each of whom knows all the others, govern the fate of the European continent, and they elect their successor from their entourage.

A FIFTEENTH CENTURY "PROTOCOL"

The principles and morality of these latter-day PROTOCOLs are as old as the tribe. Here is one of the Fifteenth Century which Jews can hardly pronounce a forgery, seeing that is taken from the Rothschild journal.

The *Revue des etudes Juives,* financed by James de Rothschild, published in 1889 two documents which showed how true the Protocols are in saying that the Learned Elders of Zion have been carrying on their plan for centuries. On January 13, 1489, Chemor, Jewish Rabbi of Arles in Provence, wrote to the Grand Sanhedrin, which had its seat in Constantinople, for advice, as the people of Arles were threatening the synagogues. What should the Jews do? This was the reply:

> "Dear Beloved brethren in Moses, we have received your letter in which you tell us of the anxieties and misfortunes which you are enduring. We are pierced by as great a pain to hear it as yourselves.
>
> "The advice of the Grand Satraps and Rabbis is the following:
>
> 1. As for what you say that the King of France obliges you to become Christians: do it, since you cannot do otherwise, but let the law of Moses be kept in your hearts.
> 2. As for what you say about the command to despoil you of your goods [the law was that on becoming converted Jews gave their possessions]; make your sons merchants, that little by little they may despoil the Christians of theirs.
> 3. As for what you say about their making attempts on your lives: make your sons doctors and apothecaries, that they may take away Christians' lives.
> 4. As for what you say of their destroying your synagogues: make your sons cannons and clerics in order that they may destroy their churches.
> 5. As for the many other vexations you complain of: arrange that your sons become advocates and lawyers, and see that they always mix

themselves up with the affairs of State, in order that by putting Christians under your yoke you may dominate the world and be avenged of them.

6. Do not swerve *from this order* that we give you, because you will bind by experience that, humiliated as your are, you will reach the actuality of power.

   Signed V.S.S.V.F.F., Prince of the Jews, 21st Caslue (November), 1489.

In the year 1844, on the eve of the Jewish Revolution of 1848, Benjamin Disraeli, whose real name was Israel, and who was a "damped", or baptized Jew, published his novel, *Conningsby*, in which occurs this ominous passage:

> "The world is governed by very different personages from what is imagined by those who are not behind the scenes."

And he went on to show that these personages were all Jews.

Now the Providence has brought to the light of day these secret Protocols all men may clearly see the hidden personages specified by Disraeli at work "behind the scenes" of all the Governments. This revelation entails on all white peoples the grave responsibility of examining and revising *au fond* their attitude towards the Race and Nation which boasts of its survival over all Empires.

NOTES

I.—"Agenture" And "The Political"

There are two words in this translation which are unusual, the words *"Agentur"* and "political" used as substantives. *"Agentur"* appears to be adopted from the original test and it means the whole body of agents and agencies directed by the Elders, whether members of the tribe or their GENTILE tools.

By "the Political" Mr Marsden meant not exactly the "body politic" but the entire machinery of politics.

II.—The Symbolic Snake of Judaism

Chapter III opens with a reference to the symbolic Snake of Judaism. In his Epilogue to the 1905 Edition of the Protocols Nilus gives the following interesting account of this symbol:

> According to the records of secret Jewish Zionism, Solomon and other JEWISH learned men had already, in 929 B.C., thought out a theoretical scheme for the peaceful conquest of the whole universe by Zion.

As history developed, this scheme was worked out in detail and completed by men who were subsequently initiated in this question. The learned men decided by peaceful means to conquer the world for Zion with the slyness of the Symbolic Snake, whose head was to represent those who have been initiated into the plans of the Jewish People - the administration was always kept secret, *even from the Jewish Nation itself.* As this Snake penetrated into the hearts of the nations which it encountered it undermined and devoured all the Non-jewish power of these States. It is foretold that the Snake has sill to finish its work, strictly adhering to the designed plan, until the course which it has to run is closed by the return of its head to Zion and until, by this means, the Snake has completed its round of Europe and has encircled it - and until, by dint of enchaining Europe, it has encompassed the whole world. This it is to accomplish by using every endeavor to subdue the other countries by an *economic* conquest.

The return of the head of the Snake to Zion can only be accomplished after the power of all the Sovereigns of Europe has been laid low, that is to say, when by means of economic crises and wholesale destruction effected everywhere, there shall have been brought about a spiritual demoralization and a moral corruption, chiefly with the assistance of Jewish Women masquerading as French, Italians, etc. These are the surest spreader of licentiousness into the lives of the leading men at the heads of nations.

A map of the course of the Symbolic Snake is shown as follows: Its first stage in Europe was in 429 B.C. in Greece, where, about the time of Pericles, the Snake first started eating into the power of that country. The second stage was in Rome in the time of Augustus, about 69 B.C. The third in Madrid in the times of Charles V, in A.D. 1552. The fourth in Paris about 1790, in the time of Louis XVI. The fifth in London from 1814 onwards (after the downfall of Napoleon). The sixth in Berlin in 1871 after the Franco-Prussian war. The seventh in St. Petersburg, over which is drawn the head of the Snake under the date 1881.

All these states which the Snake traversed have had the foundations of their constitutions shaken, Germany, with its apparent power, forming no exception to the rule. In economic conditions England and Germany are spared by the Snake, on which at present [i.e., 1905] all its efforts are concentrated. The future course of the Snake is not shown on this map, but arrows indicate its next movement towards Moscow, Kiev, and Odessa.

It is now well know to us to what extent the latter cities form the centers of the militant Jewish Race. Constantinople is shown as the last of the Snake's course before it reaches Jerusalem.

III—The term *"Goyim"*

Meaning Gentiles or Non-jew, is used throughout the Protocols and is retained by Mr. Marsden.

PROTOCOLS

OF THE MEETINGS OF THE LEARNED ELDERS OF ZION

PROTOCOL NO. 1

Right lies in Might. Freedom—an idea only. Liberalism. Gold. Faith. Self-Government. Despotism of Capital. The internal Foe. The Mob. Anarchy. Politics *versus* Morals. The Right of the strong. The Invincibility of Jew-Masonic authority. End justifies Means. The Mob a Blind Man. Political A.B.C. Party Discord. Most satisfactory form of rule—Despotism. Alcohol. Classicism. Corruption. Principles and rules of the Jew-Masonic Government. Terror. "Liberty, Equality, Fraternity." Principle of Dynastic Rule. Annihilation of the privileges of the Goy-Aristocracy (i.e., non-Jew). The New Aristocracy. The psychological calculation. Abstractness of "Liberty." Power of Removal of Representatives of the People.

.....Putting aside fine phrases we shall speak of the significance of each thought: by comparisons and deductions we shall throw light upon surrounding facts.

What I am about to set forth, then, is our system from the two point[s] of view, that of ourselves and that of the *goyim* (i.e., non-Jews).

It must be noted that men with bad instincts are more in number than the good, and therefore the best results in governing them are attained by violence and terrorization, and not by academic discussions. Every man aims at power, everyone would like to become a dictator if only he could, and rare indeed are the men who would not be willing to sacrifice the welfare of all for the sake of securing their own welfare.

What has restrained the beasts of prey who are called men? What has served for their guidance hitherto?

In the beginnings of the structure of society they were subjected to brutal and blind force; afterwards — to Law, which is the same force, only disguised. I draw the conclusion that by the law of nature right lies in force.

Political freedom is an idea but not a fact. This idea one must know how to apply whenever it appears necessary with this bait of an idea to attract the masses of the people to one's party for the purpose of crushing another who is in authority. This task is rendered easier if the opponent has himself been infected with the idea of freedom, *so-called liberalism,* and, for the sake of an idea, is willing to yield some of his power. It is precisely here that the triumph of our theory appears: the slackened reins of government are immediately, by the law of life, caught up and gathered together by a new hand, because the blind might of the nation cannot for one single day exist without guidance, and the new authority merely fits into the place of the old already weakened by liberalism.

In our day the power which has replaced that of the rulers who were liberal is the power of Gold. Time was when Faith ruled. The idea of freedom is impossible of realization because no one knows how to use it with moderation. It is enough to hand over a people to self-government for a certain length of time for that people to be turned into a disorganized mob. From that moment on we get internecine strife which soon develops into battles between classes, in the midst of which States burn down and their importance is reduced to that of a heap of ashes.

Whether a State exhausts itself in its own convulsions, whether its internal discord brings it under the power of external foes — in any case it can be accounted irretrievably lost: it is in our power. The despotism of Capital, which is entirely in our hands, reaches out to it a straw that the State, willy-nilly, must take hold of: if not — it goes to the bottom.

Should anyone of a liberal mind say that such reflections as the above are immoral I would put the following questions: — If every State has two foes and if in regard to the external foe it is allowed and not considered immoral to use every manner and art of conflict, as for example to keep the enemy in ignorance of plans of attack and defence, to attack him by night or in superior numbers, then in what way can the same means in regard to a worse foe, the destroyer of the structure of society and the commonweal, be called immoral and not permissible?

Is it possible for any sound logical mind to hope with any success to guide crowds by the aid of reasonable counsels and arguments, when any objection or contradiction, senseless though it may be, can be made and when such objection may find more favour with the people, whose powers of reasoning are superficial? Men in masses and the men of the masses, being guided solely by petty passions, paltry beliefs, customs, traditions and sentimental theorism, fall a prey to party dissension, which hinders any kind of agreement even on the basis of a perfectly reasonable argument. Every resolution of a crowd depends upon a chance or packed majority, which, in its ignorance of political secrets, put forth some ridiculous resolution that lays in the administration a seed of anarchy.

The political has nothing in common with the moral. The ruler who is governed by the moral is not a skilled politician, and is therefore unstable on his throne. He who wishes to rule must have resource both to cunning and to make-believe. Great national qualities, like frankness and honesty, are vices in politics, for they bring down rulers from their thrones more effectively and more certainly than the most powerful enemy. Such qualities must be the attributes of the kingdoms of the *goyim*, but we must in no wise be guided by them.

Our right lies in force. The word "right" is an abstract thought and proved by nothing. The word means no more than: —Give me what I want in order that thereby I may have a proof that I am stronger than you.

Where does right begin? Where does it end?

In any State in which there is a bad organization of authority, an impersonality of laws and of the rulers who have lost their personality amid the flood of rights ever multiplying out of liberalism, I find a new right — to attack by the right of the strong, and to scatter to the winds all existing forces of order and regulation, to reconstruct all institutions and to become the sovereign lord of those who have left to us the rights of their power by laying them down voluntarily in their liberalism.

Our power in the present tottering condition of all forms of power will be more invisible than any other, because it will remain invisible until the moment when it has gained such strength that no cunning can any longer undermine it.

Out of the temporary evil we are now compelled to commit will emerge the good of an unshakeable rule, which will restore the regular course of the machinery of the national life, brought to naught by liberalism. The result justifies the means. Let us, however, in our plans, direct our attention not so much to what is good and moral as to what is necessary and useful.

Before us is a plan in which is laid down strategically the line from which we cannot deviate without running the risk of seeing the labour of many centuries brought to naught.

In order to elaborate satisfactory forms of action it is necessary to have regard to the rascality, the slackness, the instability of the mob, its lack of capacity to understand and respect the conditions of its own life, or its own welfare. It must be understood that the might of a mob is blind, senseless and unreasoning force ever at the mercy of a suggestion from any side. The blind cannot lead the blind without bringing them into the abyss; consequently, members of the mob, upstarts from the people even though they should be as a genius for wisdom, yet having no understanding of the political, cannot come forward as leaders of the mob without bringing the whole nation to ruin.

Only one trained from childhood for independent rule can have understanding of the words that can be made up of the political alphabet.

A people left to itself i.e., to upstarts from its midst, brings itself to ruin by party dissensions excited by the pursuit of power and honours and the disorders arising therefrom, Is it possible for the masses of the people calmly and without petty jealousies to form judgments, to deal with the affairs of the country, which cannot be mixed up with personal interests? Can they defend themselves from an external foe? It is unthinkable, for a plan broken up into as many parts as there are heads in the mob, loses all homogeneity, and thereby becomes unintelligible and impossible of execution.

It is only with a despotic ruler that plans can be elaborated extensively and clearly in such a way as to distribute the whole properly among the several parts of the machinery of the State: from this the conclusion is inevitable that a satisfactory form of government for any country is one that concentrates in the hands of one responsible person. Without an absolute despotism there can be no existence for civilization which is carried on not by the masses but by their guide, whosoever that person may be. The mob is a savage and displays its savagery at every opportunity. The moment the mob seizes freedom in its hands it quickly turns to anarchy, which in itself is the highest degree of savagery.

Behold the alcoholized animals, bemused with drink, the right to an immoderate use of which comes along with freedom. It is not for us and ours to walk that road. The peoples of the *goyim* are bemused with alcoholic liquors; their youth has grown stupid on classicism and from early immorality, into which it has been inducted by our special agents — by tutors, lackeys, governesses in the houses of the wealthy, by clerks and others, by our women in the places of dissipation frequented by the *goyim*. In the number of these last I count also the so-called "society ladies," voluntary followers of the others in corruption and luxury.

Our countersign is — Force and Make-believe. Only force conquers in political affairs, especially if it be concealed in the talents essential to statesmen. Violence must be the principle, and cunning and make-believe the rule for governments which do not want to lay down their crowns at the feet of agents of some new power. This evil is the one and only means to attain the end, the good. Therefore we must not stop at bribery, deceit and treachery when they should serve towards the attainment of our end. In politics one must know how to seize the property of others without hesitation if by it we secure submission and sovereignty.

Our State, marching along the path of peaceful conquest, has the right to replace the horrors of war by less noticeable and more satisfactory sentences of death, necessary to maintain the terror which tends to produce blind submission. Just but merciless severity is the greatest factor of strength in the State: not only for the sake of gain but also in the name of duty, for the sake of victory, we must keep to the programme of violence and make-believe. The doctrine of squaring accounts is precisely as strong as the means of which it makes use. Therefore it is not so much by the means themselves as by the doctrine of severity that we shall triumph and bring all governments into subjection to our super-government. It is enough for them to know that we are merciless for all disobedience to cease.

Far back in ancient times we were the first to cry among the masses of the people the words "Liberty, Equality, Fraternity," words many times repeated since those days by stupid poll-parrots who from all sides round flew down upon these baits and with them carried away the well-being of the world, true freedom of the individual, formerly so well guarded against the pressure of the mob. The would-be wise men of the *goyim*, the intellectuals, could not make anything out of the uttered words in their abstractness; did not note the contradiction of their meaning and interrelation: did not see that in nature there is no equality, cannot be freedom; that Nature herself has established inequality of minds, of characters, and capacities, just as immutably as she has established subordination to her laws: never stopped to think that the mob is a blind thing, that upstarts elected from among it to bear rule are, in regard to the political, the same blind men as the mob itself, that the adept, though he be a fool, can yet rule, whereas the non-adept, even if he were a genius, understands nothing in the political — to all these things the *goyim* paid no regard; yet all the time it was based upon these things that dynastic rule rested: the father passed on to the son a knowledge of the course of political affairs in such wise that none should know it but members of the *dynasty* and none could betray it to the governed. As time went on the meaning of the dynastic transference of the true position of affairs in the political was lost, and this aided the success of our cause.

In all corners of the earth the words "Liberty, Equality, Fraternity" brought to our ranks, thanks to our blind agents, whole legions who bore our banners with enthusiasm. And all the time these words were canker-worms at work boring into the wellbeing of the *goyim*, putting an end everywhere to peace, quiet, solidarity and destroying all the foundations of the *goya* States. As you will see later, this helped us to our triumph; it gave us the possibility, among other things, of getting into our hands the master card — the destruction of the privileges, or in other words of the very existence of the aristocracy of the *goyim*, that class which was the only defense peoples and countries had against us. On the ruins of the natural and genealogical aristocracy of the *goyim* we have set up the aristocracy of our educated class headed by the aristocracy of money. The qualifications for this aristocracy we have established in wealth, which is dependent upon us, and in knowledge, for which our learned elders provide the motive force.

Our triumph has been rendered easier by the fact that in our relations with the men whom we wanted we have always worked upon the most sensitive chords of the human mind, upon the cash account, upon the cupidity, upon the insatiability for material needs of man: and each one of these human weaknesses, taken alone, is sufficient to paralyse initiative, for it hands over the will of men to the disposition of him who has bought their activities.

The abstraction of freedom has enabled us to persuade the mob in all countries that their government is nothing but the steward of the people who are the owners of the country, and that the steward may be replaced like a worn-out glove.

It is this possibility of replacing the representatives of the people which has placed them at our disposal, and, as it were, given us the power of appointment.

PROTOCOL NO. 2

Economic Wars—the foundation of the Jewish predominance. Figure-head government and "secret advisers." Successes of destructive doctrines. Adaptability in politics. Part played by the Press. Cost of gold and value of Jewish sacrifice.

It is indispensable for our purpose that wars, so far as possible, should not result in territorial gains: war will thus be brought on to the economic ground, where the nations will not fail to perceive in the assistance we give the strength of our predominance, and this state of things will put both sides at the mercy of our international *agentur;* which possesses millions of eyes ever on the watch and unhampered my any limitations whatsoever. Our international rights will then wipe out national rights, in the proper sense of right, and will rule the nations precisely as the civil law of States rules the relations of their subjects among themselves.

The administrators, whom we shall choose from among the public, with strict regard to their capacities for servile obedience, will not be persons trained in the arts of government, and will therefore easily become pawns in our game in the hands of men of learning and genius who will be their advisers, specialists bred and reared from early childhood to rule the affairs of the whole world. As is well known to you, these specialists of ours have been drawing to fit them for rule the information they need from our political plans from the lessons of history, from observations made of the events of every moment as it passes. The *goyim* are not guided by practical use of unprejudiced historical observation, but by theoretical routine without any critical regard for consequent results. We need not, therefore, take any account of them — let them amuse themselves until the hour strikes, or live on hopes of new forms of enterprising pastime, or on the memories of all they have enjoyed. For them let that play the principal part which we have persuaded them to accept as the dictates of science (theory). It is with this object in view that we are constantly, by means of our press, arousing a blind confidence in these theories. The intellectuals of the *goyim* will puff themselves up with their knowledge and without any logical verification of them will put into effect all the information available from science, which our *agentur* specialists have cunningly pieced together for the purpose of educating their minds in the direction we want.

Do not suppose for a moment that these statements are empty words: think carefully of the successes we arranged for Darwinism, Marxism, Nietzscheism. To us Jews, at any rate, it should be plain to see what a disintegrating importance these directives have had upon the minds of the *goyim*.

It is indispensable for us to take account of the thoughts, characters, tendencies of the nations in order to avoid making slips in the political and in the direction of administrative affairs. The triumph of our system, of which the component parts of the machinery may be variously disposed according to the temperament of the peoples met on our way, will fail of success if the practical application of it be not based upon a summing up of the lessons of the past in the light of the present.

In the hands of the States of to-day there is a great force that creates the movement of thought in the people, and that is the Press. The part played by the Press is to keep pointing out requirements supposed to be indispensable, to give voice to the complaints of the people, to express and create discontent. It is in the Press that the triumph of freedom of speech finds its incarnation. But the *goyim* States have not known how to make use of this force; and it has fallen into our hands. Through the Press we have gained the power to influence while remaining ourselves in the shade: thanks to the Press we have got the gold in our hands, notwithstanding that we have had to gather it out of the oceans of blood and tears. But it has paid us, though we have sacrificed many of our people. Each victim on our side is worth in the sight of God a thousand *goyim*.

PROTOCOL NO. 3

The Symbolic Snake and its significance. The instability of the constitutional scales. Terror in the palaces. Power and ambition. Parliaments "talkeries," pamphlets. Abuse of power. Economic slavery. "People's Rights." Monopolist system and the aristocracy. The Army of Mason-Jewry. Decrescence of the Goyim. Hunger and rights of capital. The mob and the coronation of "The Sovereign Lord of all the World." The fundamental precept in the programme of the future Masonic national schools. The secret of the science of the structure of society. Universal economic crisis. Security of "ours" (i.e., our people, Jews). The despotism of Masonry — the kingdom of reason. Loss of the guide. Masonry and the great French Revolution. The King Despot of the blood of Zion. Causes of the invinsibility of Masonry. Part played by secret masonic agents. Freedom.

Today I may tell you that our goal is now only a few steps off. There remains a small space to cross and the whole long path we have trodden is ready now to close its cycle of the Symbolic Snake, by which we symbolize our people. When this ring closes, all the States of Europe will be locked in its coil as in a powerful vice.

The constitution scales of these days will shortly break down, for we have established them with a certain lack of accurate balance in order that they may oscillate incessantly until they wear through the pivot on which they turn. The *goyim* are under the impression that they have welded them sufficiently strong and they have all along kept on expecting that the scales would come into equilibrium. But the pivots — the kings on their thrones — are hemmed in by their representatives, who play the fool, distraught with their own uncontrolled and irresponsible power. This power they owe to the terror which has been breathed into the palaces. As they have no means of getting at their people, into their very midst, the kings on their thrones are no longer able to come to terms with them and so strengthen themselves against seekers after power. We have made a gulf between the far-seeing Sovereign Power and the blind force of the people so that both have lost all meaning, for like the blind man and his stick, both are powerless apart.

In order to incite seekers after power to a misuse of power we have set all forces in opposition one to another, breaking up their liberal tendencies towards independence. To this end we have stirred up every form of enterprise we have armed all parties, we have set up authority as a target for every ambition. Of States we have made gladiatorial arenas where a host of confused issues contend.... A little more, and disorders and bankruptcy will be universal....

Babblers inexhaustible have turned into oratorical contests the sittings of Parliament and Administrative Boards. Bold journalists and unscrupulous pamphleteers daily fall upon executive officials. Abuses of power will put the final touch in preparing all institutions for their overthrow and everything will fly skyward under the blows of the maddened mob.

All people are chained down to heavy toil by poverty more firmly than ever they were chained by slavery and serfdom; from these, one way and another, they might free themselves, these could be settled with, but from want they will never get away. We have included in the constitution such rights as to the masses appear fictitious and not actual rights. All these so-called "People's Rights" can exist only in idea, an idea which can never be realized in practical life. What is it to the proletariat labourer, bowed double over his heavy toll, crushed by his lot in life, if talkers get the right to bable, if journalists get the right to scribble any nonsense side by side with good stuff, once the proletariat has no other profit out of the constitution save only those pitiful crumbs which we fling them from our table in return for their voting in favour of what we dictate, in favour of the men we place in power, the servants of our *agentur*....Republican rights for a poor man are no more than a bitter piece of irony, for the necessity he is under of toiling almost all day gives him no present use of them, but on the other hand robs him of all guarantee of regular and certain earnings by making him dependent on strikes by his comrades or lockouts by his masters.

The people under our guidance have annihilated the aristocracy, who were their one and only defence and fostermother for the sake of their own advantage which is inseparably bound up with the well-being of the people. Nowadays, with the destruction of the aristocracy, the people have fallen into the grips of merciless money-grinding scoundrels who have laid a pitiless and cruel yoke upon the necks of the workers.

We appear on the scene as alleged saviours of the worker from this oppression when we propose to him to enter the ranks of our fighting forces — Socialists, Anarchists, Communists — to whom we always give support in accordance with an alleged brotherly rule (of the solidarity of all humanity) of our social masonry. The aristocracy, which enjoyed by law the labour of the workers, was interested in seeing that the workers were well fed, healthy and strong. We are interested in just the opposite — in the deminution, the *killing out of the GOYIM.* Our power is in the chronic shortness of food and physical weakness of the worker because by all that this implies he is made the slave of our will, and he will not find in his own authorities either strength or energy to set against our will. Hunger creates the right of capital to rule the worker more surely than it was given to the aristocracy by the legal authority of kings.

By want and the envy and hatred which it engenders we shall move the mobs and with their hands we shall wipe out all those who hinder us on our way.

When the hour strikes for our Sovereign Lord of all the World to be crowned it is these same hands which will sweep away everything that might be a hindrance thereto.

The *goyim* have lost the habit of thinking unless prompted by the suggestions of our specialists. Therefore they do not see the urgent necessity of what we, when our kingdom comes, shall adopt at once, namely this, that *it is essential to teach in national schools one simple, true piece of knowledge, the basis of all knowledge — the knowledge of the structure of human life, of social existence, which requires division of labour, and, consequently, the division of men into classes and conditions.* It is essential for all to know that *owing to difference in the objects of human activity there cannot be any equality,* that he who by any act of his compromises a whole class cannot be equally responsible before the law with him who affects no one but only his own honour. The true knowledge of the structure of society, into the secrets of which we do not admit the *goyim*, would demonstrate to all men that the positions and work must be kept within a certain circle, that they may not become a source of human suffering, arising from an education which does not correspond with the work which individuals are called upon to do. After a thorough study of this knowledge the peoples will voluntarily submit to authority and accept such position as is appointed them in the State. In the present state of knowledge and the direction we have given to its development the people, blindly believing things in print — cherishes — thanks to promptings intended to mislead and to its own ignorance — a blind hatred towards all conditions which it considers above itself, for it has no understanding of the meaning of class and condition.

This hatred will be still further magnified by the effects of an *economic crisis,* which will stop dealings on the exchanges and bring industry to a standstill. We shall create by all the secret subterranean methods open to us and with the aid of gold, which is all in our hands, *a universal economic crisis whereby we shall throw upon the streets whole mobs of workers simultaneously in all the countries of Europe.* These mobs will rush delightedly to shed the blood of those whom, in the simplicity of their ignorance, they have envied from their cradles, and whose property they will then be able to loot.

"Ours" they will not touch, because the moment of attack will be known to us and we shall take measures to protect our own.

We have demonstrated that progress will bring all the *goyim* to the sovereignty of reason. Our despotism will be precisely that; for it will know how by wise severities to pacificate all unrest, to cauterise liberalism out of all institutions.

When the populace has seen that all sorts of concessions and indulgences are yielded it in the name of freedom it has imagined itself to be sovereign lord and has stormed its way to power, but, naturally, like every other blind man it has come upon a host of stumbling blocks, *it has rushed to find a guide, it has never had the sense to return to the former state* and it has laid down its plenipotentiary powers at our feet. Remember the French Revolution, to which it was we who gave the name of "Great": the secrets of its preparations are well known to us for it was wholly the work of our hands.

Ever since that time we have been leading the peoples from one disenchantment to another, so that in the end they should turn also from us in favour of that *King-Despot of the blood of Zion, whom we are preparing for the world.*

At the present day we are, as an international force, invincible, because if attacked by some we are supported by other States. It is the bottomless rascality of the *goyim* peoples, who crawl on their bellies to force, but are merciless towards weakness, unsparing to faults and indulgent to crimes, unwilling to bear the contradictions of a free social system but patient unto martyrdom under the violence of a bold despotism — it is those qualities which are aiding us to independence. From the premier-dictators of the present day the *goyim* peoples suffer patiently and bear such abuses as for the least of them they would have beheaded twenty kings.

What is the explanation of this phenomenon, this curious inconsequence of the masses of the peoples in their attitude towards what would appear to be events of the same order?

It is explained by the fact that these dictators whisper to the peoples through their agents that through these abuses they are inflicting injury on the States with the highest purpose — to secure the welfare of the peoples, the international brotherhood of them all, their solidarity and equality of rights. Naturally they do not tell the peoples that this unification must be accomplished only under our sovereign rule.

And thus the people condemn the upright and acquit the guilty, persuaded ever more and more that it can do whatsoever it wishes. Thanks to this state of things the people are destroying every kind of stability and creating disorders at every step.

The word "freedom" brings out the communities of men to fight against every kind of force, against every kind of authority, even against God and the laws of nature. For this reason we, when we come into our kingdom, shall have to erase this word from the lexicon of life as implying a principle of brute force which turns mobs into bloodthirsty beasts.

These beasts, it is true, fall asleep again every time when they have drunk their fill of blood, and at such times can easily be riveted into their chains. But if they be not given blood they will not sleep and continue the struggle.

PROTOCOL NO. 4

Stages of a Republic. Gentile Masonry. Freedom and Faith. International Industrial Competition. Role of Speculation. Cult of Gold.

Every republic passes through several stages. The first of these is comprised in the early days of mad raging by the blind mob, tossed hither and thither, right and left: the second is demagogy, from which is born anarchy, and that leads inevitably to despotism — not any longer legal and overt, and therefore responsible despotism, but to unseen and secretly hidden, yet nevertheless sensibly felt despotism in the hands of some secret organization or other, whose acts are the more unscrupulous inasmuch as it works behind a screen, behind the backs of all sorts of agents, the changing of whom not only does not injuriously affect but actually aids the secret force by saving it, thanks to continual changes, from the necessity of expending its resources on the rewarding of long services.

Who and what is in a position to overthrow an invisible force? And this is precisely what our force is. *Gentile* masonry blindly serves as a screen for us and our objects, but the plan of action of our force, even its very abiding place, remains for the whole people an unknown mystery.

But even freedom might be harmless and have its place in the State economy without injury to the well-being of the peoples if it rested upon the foundation of faith in God, upon the brotherhood of humanity, unconnected with the conception of equality, which is negatived by the very laws of creation, for they have established subordination. With such a faith as this a people might be governed by a wardship of parishes, and would walk contentedly and humbly under the guiding hand of its spiritual pastor submitting to the dispositions of God upon earth. This is the reason why *it is indespensable for us to undermine all faith, to tear of minds out of the GOYIM the very principle of Godhead and the spirit, and to put in its place arithmetical calculations and material needs.*

In order to give the *goyim* no time to think and take note, their minds must be diverted towards industry and trade. Thus, all the nations will be swallowed up in the pursuit of gain and in the race for it will not take note of their common foe. But again, in order that freedom may once for all disintegrate and ruin the communities of the *goyim*, we must put industry on a speculative basis: the result of this will be that what is withdrawn from the land by industry will slip through the hands and pass into speculation, that is, to our classes.

The intensified struggle for superiority and shocks delivered to economic life will create, nay, have already created, disenchanted, cold and heartless communities. Such communities will foster a strong aversion towards the higher political and towards religion. Their only guide is gain, that is Gold, which they will erect into a veritable cult, for the sake of those material delights which it can give. Then will the hour strike when, not for the sake of attaining the good, not even to win wealth, but solely out of hatred towards the privileged, the lower classes of the *goyim* will follow our lead against our rivals for power, the intellectuals of the *goyim*.

PROTOCOL NO. 5

Creation of an intensified centralization of government. Methods of seizing power by masonry. Causes of the impossibility of agreement between States. The state of "predestination" of the Jews. Gold — the engine of the machinery of States. Significance of criticism. "Show" institutions. Weariness from word-spinning. How to take a grip of public opinion. Significance of personal initiative. The Super-Government.

What form of administrative rule can be given to communities in which corruption has penetrated everywhere, communities where riches are attained only by the clever surprise tactics of semiswindling tricks; where looseness reigns: where morality is maintained by penal measures and harsh laws but not by voluntarily accepted principles: where the feelings toward faith and country are obliterated by cosmopolitan convictions? What form of rule is to be given to these communities if not that despotism which I shall describe to you later? We shall create an intensified centralization of government in order to grip in [our] hands all the forces of the community. We shall regulate mechanically all the actions of the political life of our subjects by new laws. These laws will withdraw one by one all the indulgences and liberties which have been permitted by the *goyim*, and our kingdom will be distinguished by a despotism of such magnificent proportions as to be at any moment and in every place in a position to wipe out any *goyim* who oppose us by deed or word.

We shall be told that such a despotism as I speak of is not consistent with the progress of these days, but I will prove to you that it is.

In the times when the peoples looked upon kings on their thrones as on a pure manifestation of the will of God, they submitted without a murmur to the despotic power of kings: but from the day when we insinuated into their minds the conception of their own rights they began to regard the occupants of thrones as mere ordinary mortals. The holy unction of the Lord's Anointed has fallen from the heads of kings in the eye of the people, and when we also robbed them of their faith in God the might of power was flung upon the streets into the place of public proprietorship and was seized by us.

Moreover, the art of diflecting masses and individuals by means of cleverly manipulated theory and verbiage, by regulations of life in common and all sorts of other quirks, in all which the *goyim* understand nothing, belongs likewise to the specialists of our administrative brain. Reared on analysis, observation, on delicacies of fine calculation, in this species of skill we have no rivals, any more than we have either in the drawing up of plans of political actions and solidarity. In this respect the Jesuits alone might have compared with us, but we have contrived to discredit them in the eyes of the unthinking mob as an overt organization, while we ourselves all the while have kept our secret organization in the shade. However, it is probably all the same to the world who is its sovereign lord, whether the head of Catholicism or our despot of the blood of Zion! But to us, the Chosen People, it is very far from being a matter of indifference.

For a time perhaps we might be successfully dealt with by a coalition of the GOYIM of all the world: but from this danger we are secured by the discord existing among them whose roots are so deeply seated that they can never now be plucked up. We have set one against another the personal and national reckonings of the *goyim*, religious and race hatreds, which we have fostered into a huge growth in the course of the past twenty centuries. This is the reason why there is not one State which would anywhere receive support if it were to raise its arm, for every one of them must bear in mind that any agreement against us would be unprofitable to itself. We are too strong—there is no evading our power. *The nations cannot come to even an inconsiderable private agreement without our secretly having a hand in it.*

"Per Me reges regnant". ("It is through me that Kings reign.") And it was said by the prophets that we were chosen by God Himself to rule over the whole earth. God has endowed us with genius that we may be equal to our task. Were genius in the opposite camp it would still struggle against us, but even so a newcomer is no match for the old-established settler; the struggle would be merciless between us, such a fight as the world has never yet seen. Aye, and the genius on their side would have arrived too late. All the wheels of the machinery of all States go by the force of the engine, which is in our hands, and that engine of the machinery of States is Gold. The science of political economy invented by our learned elders has for long past been giving royal prestige to capital.

Capital, if it is to co-operate untrammelled, must be free to establish a monopoly of industry and trade: this is already being put in execution by an unseen hand in all quarters of the world. This freedom will give political force to those engaged in industry, and that will help to oppress the people. Nowadays it is more important to disarm the peoples than to lead them into war; more important to use for our advantage the passions which have burst into flames than to quench their fire; more important to catch up and interpret the ideas of others to suit ourselves than to eradicate them. *The principal object of our directorate consists in this: to debilitate the public mind by criticism; to lead it away from serious reflections calculated to arouse resistance; to distract the forces of the mind towards a sham fight of empty eloquence.*

In all ages the peoples of the world, equally with individuals, have accepted words for deeds, for they are content with a show and rarely pause to note, in the public arena, whether promises are followed by performance. Therefore we shall establish show institutions which will give eloquent proof of their benefit to progress.

We shall assume to ourselves the liberal physiognomy of all parties, of all directions, and we shall give that physiognomy a voice *in orators who will speak so much that they will exhaust the patience of their hearers and produce an abhorrence of oratory.*

In order to put public opinion into our hands we must bring it into a state of bewilderment by giving expression from all sides to so many contradictory opinions and for such length of time as will suffice to make the GOYIM lose their heads in the labyrinth and come to see that the best thing is to have no opinion of any kind in matters political, which it is not given to the public to understand, because they are understood only by him who guides the public. This is the first secret.

The second secret requisite for the success of our government is comprised in the following: To multiply to such an extent national failings, habits, passions, conditions of civil life, that it will be impossible for anyone to know where he is in the resulting chaos, so that the people in consequence will fail to understand one another. This measure will also serve us in another way, namely, to sow discord in all parties, to dislocate all collective forces which are still unwilling to submit to us, and to discourage any kind of personal initiative which might in any degree hinder our affair. *There is nothing more dangerous than personal initiative;* if it has genius behind it, such initiative can do more than can be done by million, of people among whom we have sown discord. We must so direct the education of the *goyim* communities that whenever they come upon a matter requiring initiative they may drop their hands in despairing impotence. The strain which results from freedom of action saps the forces when it meets with the freedom of another. From this collision arise grave moral shocks, disenchantments, failures. *By all these means we shall so wear down the Goyim that they will be compelled to offer us international power of a nature that by its position will enable us without any violence gradually to absorb all the State forces of the world and to form a Super-Government.* In place of the rulers of to-day we shall set up a bogey which will be called the Super-Government Administration. Its hands will reach out in all directions like nippers and its organization will be of such colossal dimensions that it cannot fail to subdue all the nations of the world.

PROTOCOL NO. 6

Monopolies; upon them depend the fortunes of the *goyim*. Taking of the land out of the hands of the aristocracy. Trade, Industry and Speculation. Luxury. Rise of wages and increase of price in the articles of primary necessity. Anarchism and drunkeness. Secret meaning of the propaganda of economic theories.

We shall soon begin to establish huge monopolies, reservoirs of colossal riches, upon which even large fortunes of the *goyim* will depend to such an extent that they will go to the bottom together with the credit of the States on the day after the political smash....

You gentlemen here present who are economists, just strike an estimate of the significance of this combination!

In every possible way we must develop the significance of our Super-Government by representing it as the Protector and Benefactor of all those who voluntarily submit to us.

The aristocracy of the *goyim* as a political force, is dead - - we need not take it into account; but as landed proprietors they can still be harmful to us from the fact that they are selfsufficing in the resources upon which they live.

It is essential therefore for us at whatever cost to deprive them of their land. This object will be best attained by increasing the burdens upon landed property — in loading lands with debt. These measures will check land-holding and keep it in a state of humble and unconditional submission.

The aristocrats of the *goyim*, being hereditarily incapable of contenting themselves with little, will rapidly burn up and fizzle out.

At the same time we must intensively patronize trade and industry, but, first and foremost, speculation, the part played by which is to provide a counterpoise to industry: the absence of speculative industry will multiply capital in private hands and will serve to restore agriculture by freeing the land from indebtedness to the land banks. What we want is that industry should drain off from the land both labour and capital and by means of speculation transfer into our hands all the money of the world, and thereby throw all the *goyim* into the ranks of the proletariat. Then the *goyim* will bow down before us, if for no other reason but to get the right to exist.

To complete the ruin of the industry of the *goyim* we shall bring to the assistance of speculation the luxury which we have developed among the *goyim*, that greedy demand for luxury which is swallowing up everything. *We shall raise the rate of wages which, however, will not bring any advantage to the workers, for at the same time, we shall produce a rise in prices of the first necessaries of life, alleging that it arises from the decline of agriculture and cattle breeding: we shall further undermine artfully and deeply sources of production, by accustoming the workers to anarchy and to drunkenness and side by side therewith taking all measure to extirpate from the fact of the earth all the educated forces of the GOYIM.*

In order that the true meaning of things may not strike the GOYIM before the proper time we shall mask it under an alleged ardent desire to serve the working classes and the great principles of political economy about which our economic theories are carrying on an energetic propaganda.

PROTOCOL NO. 7

Object of the intensification of armaments. Ferments, discords and hostility all over the world. Checking the opposition of the *goyim* by wars and by a universal war. Secrecy means success in the political. The Press and public opinion. The guns of America, China and Japan.

The intensification of armaments, the increase of police forces — are all essential for the completion of the aforementioned plans. What we have to get at is that there should be in all the States of the world, besides ourselves, only the masses of the proletariat, a few millionaries devoted to our interests, police and soldiers.

Throughout all Europe, and by means of relations with Europe, in other continents also, we must create ferments, discords and hostility. Therein we gain a double advantage. In the first place we keep in check all countries, for they well know that we have the power whenever we like to create disorders or to restore order. All these countries are accustomed to see in us an indispensable force of coercion. In the second place, by our intrigues we shall tangle up all the threads which we have stretched into the cabinets of all States by means of the political, by economic treaties, or loan obligations. In order to succeed in this we must use great cunning and penetration during negotiations and agreements, but, as regards what is called the "official language," we shall keep to the opposite tactics and assume the mask of honesty and compliancy. In this way the peoples and governments of the *goyim*, whom we have taught to look only at the outside whatever we present to their notice, will still continue to accept us as the benefactors and saviours of the human race.

We must be in a position to respond to every act of opposition by war with the neighbours of that country which dares to oppose us: but if these neighbours should also venture to stand collectively together against us, then we must offer resistance by a universal war.

The principal factor of success in the political is the secrecy of its undertakings: the word should not agree with the deeds of the diplomat.

We must compel the governments of the *goyim* to take action in the direction favoured by our widely-conceived plan, already approaching the desired consummation, by what we shall represent as public opinion, secretly prompted by us through the means of that so-called "Great Power" — *the Press, which, with a few exceptions that may be disregarded, is already entirely in our hands.*

In a word, to sum up our system of keeping the governments of the *goyim* in Europe in check, we shall show our strength to one of them by terrorist attempts and to all, if we allow the possibility of a general rising against us, we shall respond with the guns of America or China or Japan.

PROTOCOL NO. 8

Ambiguous employment of juridical rights. Assistants of the Masonic directorate. Special schools and super-educational training. Economists and millionaires. To whom to entrust responsible posts in the government.

We must arm ourselves with all the weapons which our opponents might employ against us. We must search out in the very finest shades of expression and the knotty points of the lexicon of law justification for those cases where we shall have to pronounce judgments that might appear abnormally audacious and unjust, for it is important that these resolutions should be set forth in expressions that shall seem to be the most exalted moral principles cast into legal form. Our directorate must surround itself with all these forces of civilization among which it will have to work. It will surround itself with publicists, practical jurists, administrators, diplomats and, finally, with persons prepared by a special super-educational training in our special schools. These persons will have cognisance of all the secrets of the social structure, they will know all the languages that can be made up by political alphabets and words; they will be made acquainted with the whole underside of human nature, with all its sensitive chords on which they will have to play. These chords are the cast of mind of the *goyim*, their tendencies, shortcomings, vices and qualities, the particularities of classes and conditions. Needless to say that the talented assistants of authority, of whom I speak, will be taken not from among the *goyim*, who are accustomed to perform their administrative work without giving themselves the trouble to think what its aim is, and never consider what it is needed for. The administrators of the *goyim* sign papers without reading them, and they serve either for mercenary reasons or from ambition.

We shall surround our government with a whole world of economists. That is the reason why economic sciences form the principal subject of the teaching given to the Jews. Around us again will be a whole constellation of bankers, industrialists, capitalists and — *the main thing millionaires, because in substance everything will be settled by the question of figures.*

For a time, until there will no longer be any risk in entrusting responsible posts in our States to our brother Jews, we shall put them in the hands of persons whose past and reputation are such that between them and the people lies an abyss, persons who, in case of disobedience to our instructions, must face criminal charges or disappear — this in order to make them defend our interests to their last gasp.

PROTOCOL NO. 9

Application of masonic principles in the matter of reeducating the peoples. Masonic watchword. Meaning of Anti-Semitism. Dictatorship of masonry. Terror. Who are the servants of masonry. Meaning of the "clear-sighted" and the "blind" forces of the *goyim* States. Communion between authority and mob. Licence of liberalism. Seizure of education and training. False theories. Interpretation of laws. The "undergrounds" (*metropolitains*).

In applying our principles let attention be paid to the character of the people in whose country you live and act; a general, identical application of them, until such time as the people shall have been re-educated to our pattern, cannot have success. But by approaching their application cautiously you will see that not a decade will pass before the most stubborn character will change and we shall add a new people to the ranks of those already subdued by us.

The words of the liberal, which are in effect the words of our masonic watchword, namely, "Liberty, Equality, Fraternity," will, when we come into our kingdom, be changed by us into words no longer of a watchword, but only an expression of idealism, namely, into: "The right of liberty, the duty of equality, the ideal of brotherhood." That is how we shall put it, — and so we shall catch the bull by the horns..... *De facto* we have already wiped out every kind of rule except our own, although *de jure* there still remain a good many of them. Nowadays, if any States raise a protest against us it is only *pro forma* at our discretion and by our direction, for *their anti-Semitism is indispensable to us for the management of our lesser brethren.* I will not enter into further explanations, for this matter has formed the subject of repeated discussions amongst us.

For us there are no checks to limit the range of our activity. Our Super-Government subsists in extra legal conditions which are described in the accepted terminology by the energetic and forcible word — Dictatorship. I am in a position to tell you with a clear conscience that at the proper time we, the lawgivers, shall execute judgement and sentence, we shall slay and we shall spare, we, as head of all our troops, are mounted on the steed of the leader. We rule by force of will, because in our hands are the fragments of a once powerful party, now vanquished by us. *And the weapons in our hands are limitless ambitions, burning greediness, merciless vengeance, hatreds and malice.*

It is from us that the all-engulfing terror proceeds. We have in our service persons of all opinions, of all doctrines, restorating monarchists, demagogues, socialists, communists, and utopian dreamers of every kind. We have harnessed them all to the task: each one of them on his own account is boring away at the last remnants of authority, is striving to overthrow all established form of order. By these acts all States are in torture; they exhort to tranquility, are ready to sacrifice everything for peace: but we will not give them peace until they openly acknowledge our international Super-Government, and with submissiveness.

The people have raised a howl about the necessity of settling the question of Socialism by way of an international agreement. *Division into fractional parties has given them into our hands, for, in order to carry on a contested struggle one must have money, and the money is all in our hands.*

We might have reason to apprehend a union between the "clear-sighted" force of the goy kings on their thrones and the *"blind"* force of the *goy* mobs, but we have taken all the needful measure against any such possibility: between the one and the other force we have erected a bulwark in the shape of a mutual terror between them. In this way the blind force of the people remains our support and we, and we only, shall provide them with a leader and, of course, direct them along the road that leads to our goal.

In order that the hand of the blind mob may not free itself from our guiding hand, we must every now and then enter into close communion with it, if not actually in person, at any rate through some of the most trusty of our brethren. When we are acknowledged as the only authority we shall discuss with the people personally on the market places, and we shall instruct them on questions of the political in such wise as may turn them in the direction that suits us.

Who is going to verify what is taught in the village schools? But what an envoy of the government or a king on his throne himself may say cannot but become immediately known to the whole State, for it will be spread abroad by the voice of the people.

In order not to annihilate the institutions of the *goyim* before it is time we have touched them with craft and delicacy, and have taken hold of the ends of the springs which move their mechanism. These springs lay in a strict but just sense of order; we have replaced them by the chaotic license of liberalism. We have got our hands into the administration of the law, into the conduct of elections, into the press, into liberty of the person, *but principally into education and training as being the cornerstones of a free existence.*

We have fooled, bemused and corrupted the youth of the goyim by rearing them in principles and theories which are known to us to be false although it is by us that they have been inculcated.

Above the existing laws without substantially altering them, and by merely twisting them into contradictions of interpretations, we have erected something grandiose in the way of results. These results found expression first in the fact that the *interpretations masked the laws:* afterwards they entirely hid them from the eyes of the governments owing to the impossibility of making anything out of the tangled web of legislation.

This is the origin of the theory of course of arbitration.

You may say that the *goyim* will rise upon us, arms in hand, if they guess what is going on before the time comes; but in the West we have against this a manoeuvre of such appalling terror that the very stoutest hearts quail — the undergrounds, metropolitains, those subterranean corridors which, before the time comes, will be driven under all the capitals and from whence those capitals will be blown into the air with all their organizations and archives.

PROTOCOL NO. 10

The outside appearances in the political. The "genius" of rascality. What is promised by a Masonic coup d'etat? Universal suffrage. Self-importance. Leaders of Masonry. The genius who is guide of Masonry. Institutions and their functions. The poison of liberalism. Constitution a school of party discords. Era of republics. Presidents — the puppets of Masonry. Responsibility of Presidents. "Panama" Part played by chamber of deputies and president. Masonry — the legislative force. New republican constitution. Transition to masonic "despotism." Moment for the proclamation of "The Lord of all the World." Inoculation of diseases and other wiles of Masonry.

To-day I begin with a repetition of what I said before, and I beg *you to bear in mind that governments and peoples are content in the political with outside appearances.* And how, indeed, are the *goyim* to perceive the underlying meaning of things when their representatives give the best of their energies to enjoying themselves? For Our policy it is of the greatest importance to take cognisance of this detail; it will be of assistance to us when we come to consider the division of authority, freedom of speech, of the press, of religion (faith), of the law of association, of equality before the law, of the inviolability of property, of the dwelling, of taxation (the idea of concealed taxes), of the reflex force of the laws. All these questions are such as ought not to be touched upon directly and openly before the people. In cases where it is indispensable to touch upon them they must not be categorically named, it must merely be declared without detailed exposition that the principles of contemporary law are acknowledged by us. The reason of keeping silence in this respect is that by not naming a principle we leave ourselves freedom of action, to drop this or that out of it without attracting notice; if they were all categorically named they would all appear to have been already given.

The mob cherishes a special affection and respect for the geniuses of political power and accepts all their deeds of violence with the admiring response: "rascally, well, yes, it is rascally, but it's clever!...a trick, if you like, but how craftily played, how magnificently done, what impudent audacity!"...

We count upon attracting all nations to the task of erecting the new fundamental structure, the project for which has been drawn up by us. This is why, before everything, it is indispensable for us to arm ourselves and to store up in ourselves that absolutely reckless audacity and irresistible might of the spirit which in the person of our active workers will break down all hindrances on our way.

When we have accomplished our coup d'etat we shall say then to the various peoples: "Everything has gone terribly badly, all have been worn out with sufferings. We are destroying the causes of your torment — nationalities, frontiers, differences of coinages. You are at liberty, of course, to pronounce sentence upon us, but can it possibly be a just one if it is confirmed by you before you make any trial of what we are offering you." ... Then will the mob exalt us and bear us up in their hands in a unanimous triumph of hopes and expectations. Voting, which we have made the instrument will set us on the throne of the world by teaching even the very smallest units of members of the human race to vote by means of meetings and agreements by groups, will then have served its purposes and will play its part then for the last time by a unanimity of desire to make close acquaintance with us before condemning us.

To secure this we must have everybody vote without distinction of classes and qualifications, in order to establish an absolute majority, which cannot be got from the educated propertied classes. In this way, by inculcating in all a sense of self-importance, we shall destroy among the *goyim* the importance of the family and its educational value and remove the possibility of individual minds splitting off, for the mob, handled by us, will not let them come to the front nor even give them a hearing; it is accustomed to listen to us only who pay it for obedience and attention, In this way we shall create a blind, mighty force which will never be in a position to move in any' direction without the guidance of our agents set at its head by us as leaders of the mob. The people will submit to this regime because it will know that upon these leaders will depend its earnings, gratifications and the receipt of all kinds of benefits.

A scheme of government should come ready made from one brain, because it will never be clinched firmly if it is allowed to be split into fractional parts in the minds of many. It is allowable, therefore, for us to have cognisance of the scheme of action but not to discuss it lest we disturb its artfulness, the interdependence of its component parts, the practical force of the secret meaning of each clause. To discuss and make alterations in a labor of this kind by means of numerous votings is to impress upon it the stamp of all ratiocinations and misunderstandings which have failed to penetrate the depth and nexus of its plottings. We want our schemes to be forcible and suitably concocted. Therefore WE OUGHT NOT TO FLING THE WORK OF GENIUS OF OUR GUIDE to the fangs of the mob or even of a select company.

These schemes will not turn existing institutions upside down just yet. They will only affect changes in their economy and consequently in the whole combined movement of their progress, which will thus be directed along the paths laid down in our schemes.

Under various names there exists in all countries approximately one and the same thing. Representation, Ministry, Senate, State Council, Legislative and Executive Corps. I need not explain to you the mechanism of the relation of these institutions to one another, because you are aware of all that; only take note of the fact that each of the above-named institutions corresponds to some important function of the State, and I would beg you to remark that the word "important" I apply not to the institution but to the function, consequently it is not the institutions which are important but their functions. These institutions have divided up among themselves all the functions of government — administrative, legislative, executive, wherefore they have come to operate as do the organs in the human body. If we injure one part in the machinery of State, the State falls sick, like a human body, and will die.

When we introduced into the State organism the poison of Liberalism its whole political complexion underwent a change. States have been seized with a mortal illness — blood-poisoning. All that remains is to await the end of their death agony.

Liberalism produced Constitutional States, which took the place of what was the only safeguard of the *goyim*, namely, Despotism; and *a constitution, as you well know, is nothing else but a school of discords,* misunderstandings, quarrels, disagreements, fruitless party agitations, party whims —in a word, a school of everything that serves to destroy the personality of State activity. *The tribune of the "talkeries" has, no less effectively than the Press, condemned the rulers to inactivity and impotence, and thereby rendered them useless and superfluous, for which reason indeed they have been in many countries deposed. Then it was that the era of republics became possible of realization; and then it was that we replaced the ruler by a caricature of a government — by a president, taken from the mob, from the midst of our puppet creatures, our slaves.* This was the foundation of the mine which we have laid under the goy people, I should rather say, under the goy peoples.

In the near future we shall establish the responsibility of presidents.

By that time we shall be in a position to disregard forms in carrying through matters for which our impersonal puppet will be responsible. What do we care of the ranks of those striving for power should be thinned, if there should arise a deadlock from the impossibility of finding presidents, a deadlock which will finally disorganize the country? ....

In order that our scheme may produce this result we shall arrange elections in favour of such presidents as have in their past some dark, undiscovered stain, some "Panama" or other — then they will be trustworthy agents for the accomplishment of our plans out of fear of revelations and from the natural desire of everyone who has attained power, namely, the retention of the privileges, advantages and honour connected with the office of president. The chamber of deputies will provide cover for, will protect, will elect presidents, but we shall take from it the right to propose new, or make changes in existing laws, for this right will be given by us to the responsible president, a puppet in our hands. Naturally, the authority of the president will then become a target for every possible form of attack, but we shall provide him with a means of self-defense in the right of an appeal to the people, for the decision of the people over the heads of their representatives, that is to say, an appeal to that same blind slave of ours — the majority of the mob. Independently of this we shall invest the president with the right of declaring a state of war. We shall justify this last right on the ground that the president as chief of the whole army of the country must have it at his disposal, in case of need for the defense of the new republican constitution, the right to defend which will belong to him as the responsible representative of this constitution.

It is easy to understand that in these conditions the key of the shrine will lie in our hands, and no one outside ourselves will any longer direct the force of legislation.

Besides this we shall, with the introduction of the new republican constitution, take from the Chamber the right of interpellation on government measures, on the pretext of preserving political secrecy, and, further, we shall by the new constitution reduce the number of representatives to a minimum, thereby proportionately reducing political passions and the passion for politics. If, however, they should, which is hardly to be expected, burst into flame, even in this minimum, we shall nullify them by a stirring appeal and a reference to the majority of the whole people...Upon the president will depend the appointment of presidents and vice-presidents of the Chamber and the Senate. Instead of constant sessions of Parliaments we shall reduce their sittings to a few months. Moreover, the president, as chief of the executive power, will have the right to summon and dissolve Parliament, and, in the latter case, to prolong the time for the appointment of a new parliamentary assembly. But in order that the consequences of all these acts which in substance are illegal, should not, prematurely for our plans, fall upon the responsibility established by us of the president, *we shall instigate ministers and other officials of the higher administration about the president to evade his dispositions by taking measures of their own, for doing* which they will be made the scapegoats in his place....This part we especially recommend to be given to be played by the Senate, the Council of State, or the Council of Ministers, but not to an individual official.

The president will, at our discretion, interpret the sense of such of the existing laws as admit of various interpretation; he will further annul them when we indicate to him the necessity to do so, besides this, he will have the right to propose temporary laws, and even new departures in the government constitutional working, the pretext both for the one and the other being the requirements for the supreme welfare of the State.

By such measures we shall obtain the power of destroying little by little, step by step, all that at the outset when we enter on our rights, we are compelled to introduce into the constitutions of States to prepare for the transition to an imperceptible abolition of every kind of constitution, and then the time is come to turn every form of government into *our despotism.*

The recognition of our despot may also come before the destruction of the constitution; the moment for this recognition will come when the peoples, utterly wearied by the irregularities and incompetence — a matter which we shall arrange for — of their rulers, will clamour: "Away with them and give us one king over all the earth who will unite us and annihilate the causes of discords — frontiers, nationalities, religions, State debts — who will give us peace and quiet, which we cannot find under our rulers and representatives."

But you yourselves perfectly well know that *to produce the possibility of the expression of such wishes by all the nations it is indispensable to trouble in all countries the people's relations with their governments so as to utterly exhaust humanity with dissension, hatred, struggle, envy and even by the use of torture, by starvation, BY THE INOCULATION OF DISEASES, by want, so that the GOYIM see no other issue than to take refuge in our complete sovereignty in money and in all else.*

But if we give the nations of the world a breathing space the moment we long for is hardly likely ever to arrive.

PROTOCOL NO. 11

Programme of the new constitution. Certain details of the proposed revolution. The *goyim*—a pack of sheep. Secret masonry and its "show" lodges.

The State Council has been, as it were, the emphatic expression of the authority of the ruler: it will be, as the "show" part of the Legislative Corps, what may be called the editorial committee of the laws and decrees of the ruler.

This, then, is the programme of the new constitution. We shall make Law, Right and Justice (1) in the guise of proposals to the Legislative Corps, (2) by decrees of the president under the guise of general regulations, of orders of the Senate and of resolutions of the State Council in the guise of ministerial orders, (3) and in case a suitable occasion should arise — in the form of a revolution in the State.

Having established approximately the modus agendi we will occupy ourselves with details of those combinations by which we have still to complete the revolution in the course of the machinery of State in the direction already indicated. By these combinations I mean the freedom of the Press, the right of association, freedom of conscience, the voting principle, and many another that must disappear for ever from the memory of man, or undergo a radical alteration the day after the promulgation of the new constitution. It is only at that moment that we shall be able at once to announce all our orders, for, afterwards, every noticeable alteration will be dangerous, for the following reasons: if this alteration be brought in with harsh severity and in a sense of severity and limitations, it may lead to a feeling of despair caused by fear of new alterations in the same direction; if, on the other hand, it be brought in a sense of further indulgences it will be said that we have recognized our own wrongdoing and this will destroy the prestige of the infallibility of our authority, or else it will be said that we have become alarmed and are compelled to show a yielding disposition, for which we shall get no thanks because it will be supposed to be compulsory.... Both the one and the other are injurious to the prestige of the new constitution. What we want is that from the first moment of its promulgation, while the peoples of the world are still stunned by the accomplished fact of the revolution, still in a condition of terror and uncertainty, they should recognize once for all that we are so strong, so inexpungable, so superabundantly filled with power, that in no case shall we take any account of them, and so far from paying any attention to their opinions or wishes, we are ready and able to crush with irresistible power all expression or manifestation thereof at every moment and in every place, that we have seized at once everything we wanted and shall in no case divide our power with them.... Then in fear and trembling they will close their eyes to everything, and be content to await what will be the end of it all.

The *goyim* are a flock of sheep, and we are their wolves. And you know what happens when the wolves get hold of the flock?...

There is another reason also why they will close their eyes: for we shall keep promising them to give back all the liberties we have taken away as soon as we have quelled the enemies of peace and tamed all parties....

It is not worth while to say anything about how long a time they will be kept waiting for this return of their liberties...

For what purpose then have we invented this whole policy and insinuated it into the minds of the goys without giving them any chance to examine its underlying meaning? For what, indeed, if not in order to obtain in a roundabout way what is for our scattered tribe unattainable by the direct road? It is this which has served as the basis for our organization of SECRET MASONRY WHICH IS NOT KNOWN TO, AND AIMS WHICH ARE NOT EVEN SO MUCH AS SUSPECTED BY, THESE GOY CATTLE, ATTRACTED BY US INTO THE "SHOW" ARMY OF MASONIC LODGES IN ORDER TO THROW DUST IN THE EYES OF THEIR FELLOWS.

God has granted to us, His Chosen People, the gift of the dispersion, and in this which appears in all eyes to be our weakness, has come forth all our strength, which has now brought us to the threshold of sovereignty over all the world.

There now remains not much more for us to build up upon the foundation we have laid.

PROTOCOL NO. 12

Masonic interpretation of the word "freedom." Future of the press in the masonic kingdom. Control of the press. Correspondence agencies. What is progress as understood by masonry? More about the press. Masonic solidarity in the press of to-day. The arousing of "public" demands in the provinces. Infallibility of the new regime.

The word "freedom," which can be interpreted in various ways, is defined by us as follows:—

Freedom is the right to do that which the law allows. This interpretation of the word will at the proper time be of service to us, because all freedom will thus be in our hands, since the laws will abolish or create only that which is desirable for us according to the aforesaid programme.

We shall deal with the press in the following way: What is the part played by the press today? It serves to excite and inflame those passions which are needed for our purpose or else it serves selfish ends of parties. It is often vapid, unjust, mendacious, and the majority of the public have not the slightest idea what ends the press really serves. We shall saddle and bridle it with a tight curb: we shall do the same also with all productions of the printing press, for where would be the sense of getting rid of the attacks of the press if we remain targets for pamphlets and books? The produce of publicity, which nowadays is a source of heavy expense owing to the necessity of censoring it, will be turned by us into a very lucrative source of income to our State: we shall lay on it a special stamp tax and require deposits of caution-money before permitting the establishment of any organ of the press or of printing offices; these will then have to guarantee our government against any kind of attack on the part of the press. For any attempt to attack us, if such still be possible, we shall inflict fines without mercy. Such measures as stamp tax, deposits, of caution money and fines secured by these deposits, will bring in a huge income to the government. It is true that party organs might not spare money for the sake of publicity, but these we shall shut up at the second attack upon us. No one shall with impunity lay a finger on the aureole of our government infallibility. The pretext for stopping any publication will be the alleged plea that it is agitating the public mind without occasion or justification. *I beg you to note that among those making attacks upon us will also be organs established by us, but they will attack exclusively points that we have pre-determined to alter.*

Not a single announcement will reach the public without our control. Even now this is already attained by us inasmuch as all news items are received by a few agencies, in whose offices they are focused from all parts of the world. These agencies will then be already entirely ours and will give publicity only to what we dictate to them.

If already now we have contrived to possess ourselves of the minds of the *goy* communities to such an extent that they all come near looking upon the events of the world through the coloured glasses of those spectacles we are setting astride their noses: if already now there is not a single State where there exist for us any barriers to admittance into what goy stupidity calls State secrets: what will our position be then, when we shall be acknowledged supreme lords of the world in the person of our king of all the world....

Let us turn again to the *future of the printing press.* Every one desirous of being a publisher, librarian, or printer, will be obliged to provide himself with the diploma instituted therefor, which, in case of any fault, will be immediately impounded. With such measures the *instrument of thought will become an educative means in the hands of our government, which will no longer allow the mass of the nation to be led astray in by-ways and fantasies about the blessings of progress.* Is there any one of us who does not know that these phantom blessings are the direct roads to foolish imaginings which give birth to anarchical relations of men among themselves and towards authority, because progress, or rather the idea of progress, has introduced the conception of every kind of emancipation, but has failed to establish its limits.... All the so-called liberals are anarchists, if not in fact, at any rate in thought. Every one of them is hunting after phantoms of freedom, and falling exclusively into license, that is, into the anarchy of protest for the sake of protest....

We turn to the periodical press. We shall impose on it, as on all printed matter, stamp taxes per sheet and deposits of caution-money, and books of less than 30 sheets will pay double. We shall reckon them as pamphlets in order, on the one hand, to reduce the number of magazines, which are the worst form of printed poison, and, on the other, in order that this measure may force writers into such lengthy productions that they will be little read especially as they will be costly. At the same time what we shall publish ourselves to influence mental development in the direction laid down for our profit will he cheap and will be read voraciously. The tax will bring vapid literary ambitions within bounds and the liability to penalties will make literary men dependent upon us. And if there should be any found who are desirous of writing against us, they will not find any person eager to print their productions. Before accepting any production for publication in print the publisher or printer will have to apply to the authorities for permission to do so. Thus we shall know beforehand of all tricks preparing against us and shall nullify them by getting ahead with explanations on the subject treated of.

Literature and journalism are two of the most important educative forces, and therefore our government will become proprietor of the majority of the journals. This will neutralize the injurious influence of the privately-owned press and will put us in possession of the tremendous influence upon the public mind....If we give permit for ten journals, we shall ourselves found thirty, and so on the same proportion. This, however, must in nowise be suspected by the public. For which reason all journals published by us will be of the most opposite, in appearance, tendencies and opinions, thereby creating confidence in us and bringing over to us our quite unsuspicious opponents, who will thus fall into our trap and be rendered harmless.

In the front rank will stand organs of an official character. They will always stand guard over our interests, and therefore their influence will comparatively insignificant.

In the second rank will be the semi-official organs, whose part it will be to attract the tepid and indifferent.

In the third rank we shall set up our own, to all appearance, opposition, which, in at least one of its organs, will present what looks like the very antipodes to us. Our real opponents at heart will accept this simulated opposition as their own and will show us their cards.

All our newspapers will be of all possible complexions — aristocratic, republican, revolutionary, even anarchical — for so long, of course, as the constitution exists....Like the Indian idol Vishnu they will have a hundred hands, and every one of them will have a finger on any one of the public opinions as required. When a pulse quickens these hands will lead opinion in the direction of our aims, for an excited patient loses all power of judgment and easily yields to suggestion. Those fools who will think they are repeating the opinion of a newspaper of their own camp will be repeating our opinion or any opinion that seems desirable for us. In the vain belief that they are following the organ of their party they will in fact follow the flag which we hang out for them.

In order to direct our newspaper militia in this sense we must take especial and minute care in organizing this matter. Under the title of central department of the press we shall institute literary gatherings at which our agents will without attracting attention issue the orders and watchwords of the day. By discussing and controverting, but always superficially, without touching the essence of the matter, our organs will carry on a sham fight fusillade with the official newspapers solely for the purpose of giving occasion for us to express ourselves more fully than could well be done from the outset in official announcements, whenever, of course, that is to our advantage.

These attacks upon us will also serve another purpose, namely, that our subjects will be convinced of the existence of full freedom of speech and so give our agents an occasion to affirm that all organs which oppose us are empty babblers, since they are incapable of finding any substantial objections to our orders.

Methods of organization like these, imperceptible to the public eye but absolutely sure, are the best calculated to succeed in bringing the attention and the confidence of the public to the side of our government. Thanks to such methods we shall be in a position as from time to time may be required, to excite or to tranquillise the public mind on political questions, to persuade or to confuse, printing now truth, now lies, facts or their contradictions, according as they may be well or ill received, always very cautiously feeling our ground before stepping upon it....*We shall have a sure triumph over our opponents since they will not have at their disposition organs of the press in which they can give full and final expression to their views* owing to the aforesaid methods of dealing with the press. We shall not even need to refute them except very superficially.

Trial shots like these, fired by us in the third rank of our press, in case of need, will be energetically refuted by us in our semi-official organs.

Even nowadays, already, to take only the French press, there are forms which reveal masonic solidarity in acting on the watchword: all organs of the press are bound together by professional secrecy; like the augurs of old, not one of their numbers will give away the secret of his sources of information unless it be resolved to make announcement of them. Not one journalist will venture to betray this secret, for not one of them is ever admitted to practise literature unless his whole past has some disgraceful sore or other.... These sores would be immediately revealed. So long as they remain the secret of a few the prestige of the journalist attracts the majority of the country — the mob follow after him with enthusiasm.

Our calculations are especially extended to the provinces. It is indispensable for us to inflame there those hopes and impulses with which we could at any moment fall upon the capital, and we shall represent to the capitals that these expressions are the independent hopes and impulses of the provinces. Naturally, the source of them will be always one and the same — ours. What we need is that, until such time as we are in the plenitude of power, the capitals should find themselves stifled by the provincial opinion of the nation, i.e., of a majority arranged by our *agentur*. What we need is that at the psychological moment the capitals should not be in a position to discuss an accomplished fact for the simple reason, if for no other, that it has been accepted by the public opinion of a majority in the provinces.

When we are in the period of the new regime transitional to that of our assumption of full sovereignity must not admit any revelations by the press of any form of public dishonesty; it is necessary that the new regime should be thought to have so perfectly contented everybody that even criminality has disappeared.... Cases of the manifestation of criminality should remain known only to their victims and to chance witnesses — no more.

PROTOCOL NO. 13

The need for daily bread. Questions of the Political. Questions of industry. Amusements. People's Palaces. "Truth is One." The great problems.

The need for daily bread forces the *goyim* to keep silence and be our humble servants. Agents taken on to our press from among the *goyim* will at our orders discuss anything which it is inconvenient for us to issue directly in official documents, and we meanwhile, quietly amid the din of the discussion so raised, shall simply take and carry through such measures as we wish and then offer them to the public as an accomplished fact. No one will dare to demand the abrogation of a matter once settled, all the more so as it will be represented as an improvement....And immediately the press will distract the current of thought towards new questions (have we not trained people always to be seeking something new?). Into the discussions of these new questions will throw themselves those of the brainless dispensers of fortunes who are not able even now to understand that they have not the remotest conception about the matters which they undertake to discuss. Questions of the political are unattainable for any save those who have guided it already for many ages, the creators.

From all this you will see that in securing the opinion of the mob we are only facilitating the working of our machinery, and you may remark that it is not for actions but for words issued by us on this or that question that we seem to seek approval. We are constantly making public declaration that we are guided in all our undertakings by the hope, joined to the conviction, that we are serving the common weal.

In order to distract people who may be too troublesome from discussions of questions of the political we are now putting forward what we allege to be new questions of the political, namely, questions of industry. In this sphere let them discuss themselves silly! The masses are agreed to remain inactive, to take a rest from what they suppose to be political activity (which we trained them to in order to use them as a means of combatting the goy governments) only on condition of being found new employments, in which we are prescribing them something that looks like the same political object. In order that the masses themselves may not guess what they are about *we further distract them with amusements, games, pastimes, passions, people's palaces....Soon we shall begin through the press to propose competitions in art, in sport of all kinds:* these interests will finally distract their minds from questions in which we should find ourselves compelled to oppose them. Growing more and more disaccustomed to reflect and form any opinions of their own, people will begin to talk in the same tone as we, because we alone shall be offering them new directions for thought of course through such persons as will not be suspected of solidarity with us.

The part played by the liberals, utopian dreamers, will be finally played out when our government is acknowledged. Till such time they will continue to do us good service. Therefore we shall continue to direct their minds to all sorts of vain conceptions of fantastic theories, new and apparently progressive: for have we not with complete success turned the brainless heads of the *goyim* with progress, till there it not among the *goyim* one mind able to perceive that under this work lies a departure from truth in all cases where it is not a question of material inventions, for truth is one, and in it there is no place for progress. Progress, like a fallacious idea, serves to obscure truth so that none may know it except us, the Chosen of God, its guardians.

When we come into our kingdom our orators will expound great problems which have turned humanity upside down in order to bring it at the end under our beneficent rule.

Who will ever suspect then that ALL THESE PEOPLES WERE STAGE-MANAGED BY US ACCORDING TO POLITICAL PLAN WHICH NO ONE HAS SO MUCH AS GUESSED AT IN THE COURSE OF MANY CENTURIES?...

PROTOCOL NO. 14

The religion of the future. Future conditions of serfdom. Inaccessibility of knowledge regarding the religion of the future. Pornography and the printed matter of the future.

When we come into our kingdom it will be undesirable for us that there should exist any other religion than ours of the One God with whom our destiny is bound up by our position as the Chosen People and through whom our same destiny is united with the destinies of the world. We must therefore sweep away all other forms of belief. If this gives birth to the atheists whom we see to-day, it will not, being only a transitional stage, interfere with our views, but will serve as a warning for those generations which will hearken to our preaching of the religion of Moses, that, by its stable and thoroughly elaborated system has brought all the peoples of the world into subjection to us. Therein we shall emphasize its mystical right, on which, as we shall say, all its educative power is based.... Then at every possible opportunity we shall publish articles in which we shall make comparisons between our beneficent rule and those of past ages. The blessings of tranquillity, though it be a tranquility forcibly brought about by centuries of agitation, will throw into higher relief the benefits to which we shall point. The errors of the *goyim* governments will be depicted by us in the most vivid hues. We shall implant such an abhorrence of them that the peoples will prefer tranquillity in a state of serfdom to those rights of vaunted freedom which have tortured humanity and exhausted the very sources of human existence, sources which have been exploited by a mob of rascally adventurers who know not what they do.... *Useless changes of forms of government to which we instigated the GOYIM when we were undermining their state structures, will have so wearied the peoples by that time that they will prefer to suffer anything under us rather than run the risk of enduring again all the agitations and miseries they have gone through.*

At the same time we shall not omit to emphasize the historical mistakes of the goy governments which have tormented humanity for so many centuries by their lack of understanding of everything that constitutes the true good of humanity in their chase after fantastic schemes of social blessings, and have never noticed that these schemes kept on producing a worse and never a better state of the universal relations which are the basis of human life....

The whole force of our principles and methods will lie in the fact that we shall present them and expound them as a splendid contrast to the dead and decomposed old order of things in social life.

Our philosophers will discuss all the shortcomings of the various beliefs of the *goyim*, BUT NO ONE WILL EVER BRING UNDER DISCUSSION OUR FAITH FROM ITS TRUE POINT OF VIEW SINCE THIS WILL BE FULLY LEARNED BY NONE SAVE OURS, WHO WILL NEVER DARE TO BETRAY ITS SECRETS.

In countries known as progressive and enlightened we have created a senseless, filthy, abominable literature. For some time after our entrance to power we shall continue to encourage its existence in order to provide a telling relief by contrast to the speeches, party programme, which will be distributed from exalted quarters of ours. Our wise men, trained to become leaders of the *goyim*, will compose speeches, projects, memoirs, articles, which will be used by us to influence the minds of the *goyim*, directing them towards such understanding and forms of knowledge as have been determined by us.

PROTOCOL NO. 15

One-day coup d'etat (revolution) over all the world. Executions. Future lot of *goyim*-masons. Mysticism of authority. Multiplication of masonic lodges. Central governing board of masonic elders. The "Azev-tactics." Masonry as leader and guide of all secret societies. Significance of public applause. Collectivism. Victims. Executions of masons. Fall of the prestige of laws and authority. Our position as the Chosen people. Brevity and clarity of the laws of the kingdom of the future. Obedience to orders. Measures against abuse of authority. Severity of penalties. Age-limit for judges. Liberalism of judges and authorities. The money of all the world. Absolutism of masonry. Right of appeal. Patriarchal "outside appearance" of the power of the future "ruler." Apotheosis of the ruler. The right of the strong as the one and only right. The King of Israel. Patriarch of all the world.

When we at last definitely come into our kingdom by the aid of *coups d'etat* prepared everywhere for one and the same day, after the worthlessness of all existing forms of government has been definitely acknowledged (and not a little time will pass before that comes about, perhaps even a whole century) we shall make it our task to see that against us such things as plots shall no longer exist. With this purpose we shall slay without mercy all who take arms (in hand) to oppose our coming into our kingdom. Every kind of new institution of anything like a secret society will also be punished with death; those of them which are now in existence, are known to us, serve us and have served us, we shall disband and send into exile to continents far removed from Europe. *In this way we shall proceed with those GOY masons who know too much;* such of these as we may for some reason spare will be kept in constant fear of exile. We shall promulgate a law making all former members of secret societies liable to exile from Europe as the centre of our rule.

Resolutions of our government will be final, without appeal.

In the *goy* societies, in which we have planted and deeply rooted discord and protestantism, the only possible way of restoring order is to employ merciless measures that prove the direct force of authority: no regard must be paid to the victims who fall, they suffer for the well being of the future. The attainment of that well-being, even at the expense of sacrifices, is the duty of any kind of government that acknowledges as justification for its existence not only its privileges but its obligations. The principal guarantee of stability of rule is to confirm the aureole of power, and this aureole is attained only by such a majestic inflexibility of might as shall carry on its face the emblems of inviolability from mystical causes — from the choice of God. Such was, until recent times, the Russian autocracy, the one and only serious foe we had in the world, without counting the Papacy. Bear in mind the example when Italy, drenched with blood, never touched a hair of the head of Sulla who had poured forth that blood: Sulla enjoyed an apotheosis for his might in the eyes of the people, though they had been torn in pieces by him, but his intrepid return to Italy ringed him round with inviolability. The people do not lay a finger on him who hypnotizes them by his daring and strength of mind.

Meantime, however, until we come into our kingdom, we shall act in the contrary way: we shall create and multiply free masonic lodges in all the countries of the world, absorb into them all who may become or who are prominent in public activity, for in these lodges we shall find our principal intelligence office and means of influence. All these lodges we shall bring under one central administration, known to us alone and to all others absolutely unknown, which will be composed of our learned elders. The lodges will have their representatives who will serve to screen the above-mentioned administration of *masonry* and from whom will issue the watchword and programme. In these lodges we shall tie together the knot which binds together all revolutionary and liberal elements. Their composition will be made up of all strata of society. The most secret political plots will be known to us and will fall under our guiding hands on the very day of their conception. *Among the members of these lodges will be almost all the agents of international and national police* since their service is for us irreplaceable in the respect that the police is in a position not only to use its own particular measures with the insubordinate, but also to screen our activities and provide pretexts for discontents, et cetera.

The class of people who most willingly enter into secret societies are those who live by their wits, careerists, and in general people, mostly light-minded, with whom we shall have no difficulty in dealing and in using to wind up the mechanism of the machine devised by us. If this world grows agitated the meaning of that will be that we have had to stir it up in order to break up its too great solidarity. *But if there should arise in its midst a plot, then at the head of that plot will be no other than one of our most trusted servants.* It is natural that we and no other should lead *masonic* activities, for we know whither we are leading, we know the final goal of every form of activity whereas the *goyim* have knowledge of nothing, not even of the immediate effect of action; they put before themselves, usually, the momentary reckoning of the satisfaction of their self-opinion in the accomplishment of their thought without even remarking that the very conception never belonged to their initiative but to our instigation of their thought....

The *goyim* enter the lodges out of curiosity or in the hope by their means to get a nibble at the public pie, and some of them in order to obtain a hearing before the public for their impracticable and groundless fantasies: they thirst for the emotion of success and applause, of which we are remarkably generous. And the reason why we give them this success is to make use of the high conceit of themselves to which it gives birth, for that insensibly disposes them to assimilate our suggestions without being on their guard against them in the fullness of their confidence that it is their own infallibility which is giving utterance to their own thoughts and that it is impossible for them to borrow those of others.... You cannot imagine to what extent the wisest of the *goyim* can be brought to a state of unconscious naivete in the presence of this condition of high conceit of themselves, and at the same time how easy it is to take the heart out of them by the slightest ill-success, though it be nothing more than the stoppage of the applause they had, and to reduce them to a slavish submission for the sake of winning a renewal of success....*By so much as ours disregard success if only they can carry through their plans. By so much the GOYIM are willing to sacrifice any plans only to have success.* This psychology of theirs materially facilitates for us the task of setting them in the required direction. These tigers in appearance have the souls of sheep and the wind blows freely through their heads. We have set them on the hobby-horse of an idea about the absorption of individuality by the symbolic unit of *collectivism*....They have never yet and they never will have the sense to reflect that this hobby horse is a manifest violation of the most important law of nature, which has established from the very creation of the world one unit unlike another and precisely for the purpose of instituting individuality.

If we have been able to bring them to such a pitch of stupid blindness is it not a proof, and an amazingly clear proof, of the degree to which the mind of the *goyim* is undeveloped in comparison with our mind? This it is, mainly, which guarantees our success.

And how far-seeing were our learned elders in ancient times when they said that to attain a serious end it behooves not to stop at any means or to count the victims sacrificed for the sake of that end.... We have not counted the victims of the seed of the goy cattle, though we have sacrificed many of our own, but for that we have now already given them such a position on the earth as they could not even have dreamed of. The comparatively small numbers of the victims from the number of ours have preserved our nationality from destruction.

Death is the inevitable end for all. It is better to bring that end nearer to those who hinder our affairs than to ourselves, to the founders of this affair. *We execute masons in such wise that none save the brotherhood can ever have a suspicion of it, not even the victims themselves of our death sentence, they all die when required as if from a normal kind of illness.*...Knowing this, even the brotherhood in its turn dare not protest. By such methods we have plucked out of the midst of masonry the very root of protest against our disposition. While preaching liberalism to the *goyim* we at the same time keep our own people and our agents in a state of unquestioning submission.

Under our influence the execution of the laws of the *goyim* has been reduced to a minimum. The prestige of the law has been exploded by the liberal interpretations introduced into this sphere. In the most important and fundamental affairs and questions judges decide as we dictate to them, see matters in the light wherewith we enfold them for the administration of the *goyim*, of course, through persons who are our tools though we do not appear to have anything in common with them — by newspaper opinion or by other means.... Even senators and the higher administration accept our counsels. The purely brute mind of the *goyim* is incapable of use for analysis and observation, and still more for the foreseeing whither a certain manner of setting a question may tend.

In this difference in capacity for thought between the *goyim* and ourselves may be clearly discerned the seal of our position on the Chosen People and of our higher quality of humanness, in contra-distinction to the brute mind of the *goyim*. Their eyes are open, but see nothing before them and do not invent (unless, perhaps, material things). From this it is plain that nature herself has destined us to guide and rule the world.

When comes the time of our overt rule, the time to manifest its blessings, we shall remake all legislatures, all our laws will be brief, plain, stable, without any kind of interpretations, so that anyone will be in a position to know them perfectly. The main feature which will run right through them is submission to orders, and this principle will be carried to a grandiose height. Every abuse will then disappear in consequence of the responsibility of all down to the lowest unit before the higher authority of the representative of power. Abuses of power subordinate to this last instance will be so mercilessly punished that none will be found anxious to try experiments with their own powers. We shall follow up jealously every action of the administration on which depends the smooth running of the machinery of the State, for slackness in this produces slackness everywhere; not a single case of illegality or abuse of power will be left without exemplary punishment.

Concealment of guilt, connivance between those in the service of the administration — all this kind of evil will disappear after the very first examples of severe punishment. The aureole of our power demands suitable, that is, cruel, punishments for the slightest infringement, for the sake of gain, of its supreme prestige. The sufferer, though his punishment may exceed his fault, will count as a soldier falling on the administrative field of battle in the interest of authority, principle and law, which do not permit that any of those who hold the reins of the public coach should turn aside from the public highway to their own private paths. *For example: our judges will know that whenever they feel disposed to plume themselves on foolish clemency they are violating the law of justice which is instituted for the exemplary edification of men by penalties for lapses and not for display of the spiritual qualities of the judge....* Such qualities it is proper to show in private life, but not in a public square which is the educationary basis of human life.

Our legal staff will serve not beyond the age of 55, firstly because old men more obstinately hold to prejudiced opinions, and are less capable of submitting to new directions, and secondly because this will give us the possibility by this measure of securing elasticity in the changing of staff, which will thus the more easily bend under our pressure: he who wishes to keep his place will have to give blind obedience to deserve it. In general, our judges will be elected by us only from among those who thoroughly understand that the part they have to play is to punish and apply laws and not to dream about the manifestations of liberalism at the expense of the educationary scheme of the State, as the *goyim* in these days imagine it to be.... This method of shuffling the staff will serve also to explode any collective solidarity of those in the same service and will bind all to the interests of the government upon which their fate will depend. The young generation of judges will be trained in certain views regarding the inadmissibility of any abuses that might disturb the established order of our subjects among themselves.

In these days the judges of the *goyim* create indulgences to every kind of crimes, not having a just understanding of their office, because the rulers of the present age in appointing judges to office take no care to inculcate in them a sense of duty and consciousness of the matter which is demanded of them. As a brute beast lets out its young in search of prey, so do the *goyim* give their subjects places of profit without thinking to make clear to them for what purpose such place was created. This is the reason why their governments are being ruined by their own forces through the acts of their own administration.

Let us borrow from the example of the results of these actions yet another lesson for our government.

We shall root out liberalism from all the important strategic posts of our government on which depends the training of subordinates for our State structure. Such posts will fall exclusively to those who have been trained by us for administrative rule. To the possible objection that the retirement of old servants will cost the Treasury heavily, I reply, firstly, they will be provided with some private service in place of what they lose, and, secondly, I have to remark that all the money in the world will be concentrated in our hands, consequently it is not our government that has to fear expense.

Our absolutism will in all things be logically consecutive and therefore in each one of its decrees our supreme will will be respected and unquestionably fulfilled: it will ignore all murmurs, all discontents of every kind and will destroy to the root every kind of manifestation of them in act by punishment of an exemplary character.

We shall abolish the right of cassation, which will be transferred exclusively to our disposal — to the cognisanze of him who rules, for we must not allow the conception among the people of a thought that there could be such a thing as a decision that is not right of judges set up by us. If, however, anything like this should occur, we shall ourselves cassate the decision, but inflict therewith such exemplary punishment on the judge for lack of understanding of his duty and the purpose of his appointment as will prevent a repetition of such cases. I repeat that it must be borne in mind that we shall know every step of our administration which only needs to be closely watched for the people to be content with us, for it has the right to demand from a good government a good official.

Our government will have the appearance of a patriarchal paternal guardianship on the part of our ruler. Our own nation and our subjects will discern in his person a father caring for their every need, their every act, their every inter-relation as subjects one with another, as well as their relations to the ruler. They will then be so thoroughly imbued with the thought that it is impossible for them to dispense with this wardship and guidance, if the wish to live in piece and quiet, *that they will acknowledge the autocracy of* our ruler with a devotion bordering on APOTHEOSIS, especially when they are convinced that those whom we set up do not put their own in place of his authority, but only blindly execute his dictates. They will be rejoiced that we have regulated everything in their lives as is done by wise parents who desire to train their children in the cause of duty and submission, For the peoples of the world in regard to the secrets of our polity are ever through the ages only children under age, precisely as are also their governments.

As you see, I found our despotism on right and duty: the right to compel the execution of duty is the direct obligation of a government which is a father for its subjects. It has the right of the strong that it may use it for the benefit of directing humanity towards that order which is defined by nature, namely, submission. Everything in the world is in a state of submission, if not to man, then to circumstances or its own inner character, in all cases, to what is stronger. And so shall we be this something stronger for the sake of good.

We are obliged without hesitation to sacrifice individuals, who commit a breach of established order, for in the exemplary punishment of evil lies a great educational problem.

When the King of Israel sets upon his sacred head the crown offered him by Europe he will become patriarch of the world. The indispensable victims offered by him in consequence of their suitability will never reach the number of victims offered in the course of centuries by the mania of magnificence, the emulation between the goy governments.

Our King will be in constant communion with the peoples, making to them from the tribune speeches which fame will in that same hour distribute over all the world.

PROTOCOL NO. 16

Emasculation of the universities. Substitute for classicism. Training and calling. Advertisement of the authority of "the ruler" in the schools. Abolition of freedom of instruction. New Theories. Independence of thought. Teaching by object lessons.

In order to effect the destruction of all collective forces except ours we shall emasculate the first stage of collectivism—the universities, by re-educating them in a new direction. *Their officials and professors will be prepared for their business by detailed secret programmes of action from which they will not with immunity diverge, not by one iota. They will be appointed with especial precaution, and will be so placed as to be wholly dependent upon the Government.*

We shall exclude from the course of instruction State Law as also all that concerns the political question. These subjects will be taught to a few dozens of persons chosen for their preeminent capacities from among the number of the initiated. *The universities must no longer send out from their halls milksops concocting plans for a constitution, like a comedy or a tragedy, busying themselves with questions of policy in which even their own fathers never had any power of thought.*

The ill-guided acquaintance of a large number of persons with questions of polity creates utopian dreamers and bad subjects, as you can see for yourselves from the example of the universal education in this direction of the *goyim*. We must introduce into their education all those principles which have so brilliantly broken up their order. But when we are in power we shall remove every kind of disturbing subject from the course of education and shall make out of the youth obedient children of authority, loving him who rules as the support and hope of peace and quiet.

Classicism, as also any form of study of ancient history, in which there are more bad than good examples, we shall replace with the study of the programme of the future. We shall erase from the memory of men all facts of previous centuries which are undesirable to us, and leave only those which depict all the errors of the governments of the *goyim*. The study of practical life, of the obligations of order, of the relations of people one to another, of avoiding bad and selfish examples which spread the infection of evil, and similar questions of an educative nature, will stand in the forefront of the teaching programme, which will be drawn up on a separate plan for each calling or slate of life, in no wise generalising the teaching. This treatment of the question has special importance.

Each state of life must be trained within strict limits corresponding to its destination and work in life. *The occasional genius has always managed and always will manage to slip through into other states of life but it is the most perfect folly for the sake of this rare occasional genius to let through into ranks foreign to them the untalented who thus rob of their places those who belong to those ranks by birth or employment. You know yourselves in what all this has ended for the goyim who allowed this crying absurdity.*

In order that he who rules may be seated firmly in the hearts and minds of his subjects it is necessary for the time of his activity to instruct the whole nation in the schools and on the market places about his meaning and his acts and all his beneficent initiatives.

We shall abolish every kind of freedom of instruction. Learners of all ages will have the right to assemble together with their parents in the educational establishments as it were in a club: during these assemblies, on holydays, teachers will read what will pass as free lectures on questions of human relations, of the laws of examples, of the limitations which are born of unconscious relations, and, finally, of the philosophy of new theories not yet declared to the world. These theories will be raised by us to the stage of a dogma of faith as a transitional stage towards our faith. On the completion of this exposition of our programme of action in the present and the future I will read you the principles of these theories.

In a word, knowing by the experience of many centuries that people live and are guided by ideas, that these ideas are imbibed by people only by the aid of education provided with equal success for all ages of growth, but of course by varying methods, we shall swallow up and confiscate to our own use the last scintilla of independence of thought, which we have for long past been directing towards subjects and ideas useful for us. The system of bridling thought is already at work in the so-called system of teaching by object lessons, the purpose of which is to turn the *goyim* into unthinking submissive brutes waiting for things to be presented before their eyes in order to form an idea of them....In France, one of four best agents, Bourgeois, has already made public a new programme of teaching by object lessons.

PROTOCOL NO. 17

Advocacy. Influence of the priesthood of the *goyim*. Freedom of conscience. Papal Court. King of the Jews as Patriarch-Pope. How to fight the existing Church. Function of contemporary press. Organization of police. Volunteer police. Espionage on the pattern of the kabal espionage. Abuses of authority.

The practice of advocacy produces men cold, cruel, persistent, unprincipled, who in all cases take up an impersonal purely legal standpoint. They have the inveterate habit to refer everything to its value for the defence, not to the public welfare of its results. They do not usually decline to undertake any defence whatever, they strive for an acquittal at all costs, cavilling over every petty crux of jurisprudence and thereby they demoralize justice. For this reason we shall set this profession into narrow frames which will keep it inside this sphere of executive public service. Advocates, equally with judges, will be deprived of the right of communication with litigants; they will receive business only from the court and will study it by notes off report and documents, defending their clients after they have been interrogated in court on facts that have appeared. They will receive an honorarium without regard to the quality of the defence. This will render them mere reporters on law-business in the interests of justice and as counterpoise to the proctor who will be the reporter in the interests of prosecution; this will shorten business before the courts. In this way will be established a practice of honest unprejudiced defence conducted not from personal interest but by conviction. This will also, by the way, remove the present practice of corrupt bargain between advocates to agree only to let that side win which pays most....

We have long past taken care to discredit the priesthood of the goyim, and thereby to ruin their mission on earth which in these days might still be a great hindrance to us. Day by day its influence on the peoples of the world is falling lower. *Freedom of conscience has been declared everywhere, so that now only years divide us from the moment of the complete wrecking of that Christian religion,* as to other religions we shall have still less difficulty in dealing with them, but it would be premature to speak of this now. We shall set clericalism and clericals into such narrow frames as to make their influence move in retrogressive proportion to its former progress.

When the time comes finally to destroy the papal court the finger of an invisible hand will point the nations towards this court. When, however, the nations fling themselves upon it, we shall come forward in the guise of its defenders as if to save excessive bloodshed. By this diversion we shall penetrate to its very bowels and be sure we shall never come out again until we have gnawed through the entire strength of this place.

The King of the Jews will be the real Pope of the Universe, the patriarch of an international Church.

But, *in the meantime,* while we are re-educating youth in new traditional religions and afterwards in ours, *we shall not overtly lay a finger on existing churches but we shall fight against them by criticism calculated to produce schism....*

In general, then, our contemporary press will continue to convict State affairs, religions, incapacities of the *goyim*, always using the most unprincipled expressions in order by every means to lower their prestige in the manner which can only be practiced by the genius of our gifted tribe....

Our kingdom will be an apologia of the divinity Vishnu, in whom is found its personification — in our hundred hands will be, one in each, the springs of the machinery of social life. We shall see everything without the aid of official police which, in that scope of its rights which we elaborated for the use of the *goyim*, hinders governments from seeing. In our programme *one-third of our subjects will keep the rest under observation* from a sense of duty, on the principle of volunteer service to the State. It will then be no disgrace to be a spy and informer, but a merit: unfounded denunciations, however, will be cruelly punished that there may be no development of abuses of this right.

Our agents will be taken from the higher as well as the lower ranks of society, from among the administrative class who spend their time in amusements, editors, printers and publishers, booksellers, clerks, and salesmen, workmen, coachmen, lackeys, et cetera. This body, having no rights and not being empowered to take any action on their own account, and consequently a police without any power, will only witness and report: verification of their reports and arrests will depend upon a responsible group of controllers of police affairs, while the actual act of arrest will be performed by the gendarmerie and the municipal police. Any person not denouncing anything seen or heard concerning questions of polity will also be charged with and made responsible for concealment, if it be proved that he is guilty of this crime.

Just as nowadays our brethren are obliged at their own risk to denounce to the kabal apostates of their own family or members who have been noticed doing anything in opposition to the *kabal, so in our kingdom over all the world it will be obligatory for all our subjects to observe the duty of service to the State in this direction.*

Such an organization will extirpate abuses of authority, of force, of bribery, everything in fact which we by our counsel, by our theories of the superhuman rights of man, have introduced into the customs of the *goyim*....But how else were we to procure that increase of causes predisposing to disorders in the midst of their administration?...Among the number of those methods one of the most important is — agents for the restoration of order, so placed as to have the opportunity in their disintegrating activity of developing and displaying their evil inclinations — obstinate self-conceit, irresponsible exercise of authority, and, first and foremost, venality.

PROTOCOL NO. 18

Measures of secret defense. Observation of conspiracies from the inside. Overt secret defense — the ruin of authority, Secret defense of the King of the Jews. Mystical prestige of authority. Arrest on the first suspicion.

When it becomes necessary for us to strengthen the strict measures of secret defense (the most fatal poison for the prestige of authority) we shall arrange a simulation of disorders or some manifestation of discontents finding expression through the co-operation of good speakers. Round these speakers will assemble all who are sympathetic to his utterances. This will give us the pretext for domiciliary perquisitions and surveillance on the part of our servants from among the number of the *goyim* police....

As the majority of conspirators act out of love for the game, for the sake of talking, so, until they commit some overt act we shall not lay a finger on them but only introduce into their midst observation elements. . . It must be remembered that the prestige of authority is lessened if it frequently discovers conspiracies against itself: this implies a presumption of consciousness of weakness, or, what is still worse, of injustice. You are aware that we have broken the prestige of the goy kings by frequent attempts upon their lives through our agents, blind sheep of our flock, who are easily moved by a few liberal phrases to crimes provided only they be painted in political colours. *We have compelled the rulers to acknowledge their weakness in advertising overt measures of secret defence and thereby we shall bring the promise of authority to destruction.*

Our ruler will be secretly protected only by the most insignificant guard, because we shall not admit so much as a thought that there could exist against him any sedition with which he is not strong enough to contend and is compelled to hide from it.

If we should admit this thought, as the *goyim* have done and are doing, we should ipso facto be signing a death sentence, if not for our ruler, at any rate for his dynasty, at no distant date.

According to strictly enforced outward appearances our ruler will employ his power only for the advantage of the nation and in no wise for his own or dynastic profits. Therefore, with the observance of this decorum, his authority will be respected and guarded by the subjects themselves, it will receive an apotheosis in the admission that with it is bound up the well-being of every citizen of the State, for upon it will depend all order in the common life of the pack.

Overt defense of the kind argues weakness in the organization of his strength.

Our ruler will always among the people be surrounded by a mob of apparently curious men and women, who will occupy the front ranks about him, to all appearance by chance, and will restrain the ranks the rest out of respect as it will appear for good order. This will sow an example of restraint also in others. If a petitioner appears among the people trying to hand a petition and forcing his way through the ranks, the first ranks must receive the petition and before the eyes of the petitioner pass it to the ruler, so that all may know that what is handed in reaches its destination, that, consequently, there exists a control of the ruler himself. The aureole of power requires for its existence that the people may be able to say: "If the king knew of this," or: "the king will hear of it."

With the establishment of official secret defense the mystical prestige of authority disappears: given a certain audacity, and everyone counts himself master of it, the seditionmonger is conscious of his strength, and when occasion serves watches for the moment to make an attempt upon authority....For the *goyim* we have been preaching something else, but by that very fact we are enabled to see what measures of overt defense have brought them to....

Criminals with us will be arrested at the first more or less well-grounded suspicion; it cannot be allowed that out of fear of a possible mistake an opportunity should be given of escape to persons suspected of a political lapse or crime, for in these matters we shall be literally merciless. If it is still possible, by stretching a point, to admit a reconsideration of the motive causes in simple crime, there is no possibility of excuse for persons occupying themselves with questions in which nobody except the government can understand anything....And it is not all governments that understand true policy.

PROTOCOL NO. 19

The right of presenting petitions and projects. Sedition. Indictment of political crimes. Advertisement of political crimes.

If we do not permit any independent dabbling in the political we shall on the other hand encourage every kind of report or petition with proposals for the government to examine into all kinds of projects for the amelioration of the condition of the people; this will reveal to us the defects or else the fantasies of our subjects, to which we shall respond either by accomplishing them or by a wise rebutment to prove the shortsightedness of one who judges wrongly.

Sedition-mongering is nothing more than the yapping of a lap-dog at an elephant. For a government well organized, not from the police but from the public point of view, the lap-dog yaps at the elephant in entire unconsciousness of its strength and importance. It needs no more than to take a good example to show the relative importance of both and the lap-dogs will cease to yap and will wag their tails the moment they set eyes on an elephant.

In order to destroy the prestige of heroism for political crime we shall send it for trial in the category of thieving, murder, and every kind of abominable and filthy crime. Public opinion will then confuse in its conception this category of crime with the disgrace attaching to every other and will brand it with the same contempt.

We have done our best, and I hope we have succeeded to obtain that the *goyim* should not arrive at this mean of contending with sedition. It was for this reason that through the Press and in speeches, indirectly — in cleverly compiled schoolbooks on history, we have advertised the martyrdom alleged to have been accepted by sedition-mongers for the idea of the commonweal. This advertisement has increased the contingent of liberals and has brought thousands of *goyim* into the ranks of our livestock cattle.

PROTOCOL NO. 20

FINANCIAL PROGRAMME. Progressive tax. Stamp progressive taxation. Exchequer, interest-bearing papers and stagnation of currency. Method of accounting. Abolition of ceremonial displays. Stagnation of capital. Currency issue. Gold standard. Standard of cost of working man power. Budget. State loans. One per cent interest series. Industrial shares. Rulers of the *goyim*: courtiers and favouritism, masonic agents.

To-day we shall touch upon the financial programme, which I put off to the end of my report as being the most difficult, the crowning and the decisive point of our plans. Before entering upon it I will remind you that I have already spoken before by way of a hint when I said that the sum total of our actions is settled by the question of figures.

When we come into our kingdom our autocratic government will avoid, from a principle of self-preservation, sensibly burdening the masses of the people with taxes, remembering that it plays the part of father and protector. But as State organization costs dear it is necessary nevertheless to obtain the funds required for it. It will, therefore, elaborate with particular precaution the question of equilibrium in this matter.

Our rule, in which the king will enjoy the legal fiction that everything in his State belongs to him (which may easily be translated into fact), will be enabled to resort to the lawful confiscation of all sums of every kind for the regulation of their circulation in the State. From this follows that taxation will best be covered by a progressive tax on property. In this manner the dues will be paid without straitening or ruining anybody in the form of a percentage of the amount of property. The rich must be aware that it is their duty to place a part of their superfluities at the disposal of the State since the State guarantees them security of possession of the rest of their property and the right of honest gains, I say honest, for the control over property will do away with robbery on a legal basis.

This social reform must come from above, for the time is ripe for it — it is indispensable as a pledge of peace.

The tax upon the poor man is a seed of revolution and works to the detriment of the state which in hunting after the trifling is missing the big. Quite apart from this, a tax on capitalists diminishes the growth of wealth in private hands in which we have in these days concentrated it as a counterpoise to the government strength of the *goyim* — their State finances.

A tax increasing in a percentage ratio to capital will give a much larger venue than the present individual or property tax, which is useful to us now for the sole reason that it excites trouble and discontent among the *goyim*.

The force upon which our king will rest consist in the equilibrium and the guarantee of peace, for the sake of which things it is indispensable that the capitalists should yield up a portion of their incomes for the sake of the secure working of the machinery of the State. State needs must be paid by those who will not feel the burden and have enough to take from.

Such a measure will destroy the hatred of the poor man for the rich, in whom he will see a necessary financial support for the State, will see in him the organizer of peace and well-being since he will see that it is the rich man who is paying the necessary means to attain these things.

In order that payers of the educated classes should not too much distress themselves over the new payments they will have full accounts given them of the destination of those payments, with the exception of such sums as well be appropriated for the needs of the throne and the administrative institutions.

He who reigns will not have any properties of his own once all in the State represents his patrimony, or else the one would be in contradiction to the other; the fact of holding private means would destroy the right of property in the common possessions of all.

Relatives of him who reigns, his heirs excepted, who will be maintained by the resources of the State, must enter the ranks of servants of the State or must work to obtain the right to property; the privilege of royal blood must not serve for the spoiling of the treasury.

Purchase, receipt of money or inheritance will be subject to the payment of a stamp progressive tax. Any transfer of property, whether money or other, without evidence of payment of this tax which will be strictly registered by names, will render the former holder liable to pay interest on the tax from the moment of transfer of these sums up to the discovery of his evasion of declaration of the transfer. Transfer documents must be presented weekly at the local treasury office with notifications of the name, surname and permanent place of residence of the former and the new holder of the property. This transfer with register of names must begin from a definite sum which exceeds the ordinary expenses of buying and selling of necessaries, and these will be subject to payment only by a stamp impost of a definite percentage of the unit.

Just strike an estimate of how many times such taxes as these will cover the revenue of the *goyim* States.

The State exchequer will have to maintain a definite complement of reserve sums, and all that is collected above that complement must be returned into circulation. On these sums will be organized public works. The initiative in works of this kind, proceeding from State sources, will bind the working class firmly to the interests of the State and to those who reign. From these same sums also a part will be set aside as rewards of inventiveness and productiveness.

On no account should so much as a single unit above the definite and freely estimated sums be retained in the State treasuries, for money exists to be circulated and any kind of stagnation of money acts ruinously on the running of the State machinery, for which it is the lubricant; a stagnation of the lubricant may stop the regular working of the mechanism.

The substitution of interest-bearing paper for a part of the token of exchange has produced exactly this stagnation. The consequences of this circumstance are already sufficiently noticeable.

A court of account will also be instituted by us and in it the ruler will find at any moment a full accounting for State income and expenditure, with the exception of the current monthly account, not yet made up, and that of the preceding month, which will not yet have been delivered.

The one and only person who will have no interest in robbing the State is its owner, the ruler. This is why his personal control will remove the possibility of leakages of extravagances.

The representative function of the ruler at receptions for the sake of etiquette, which absorbs so much invaluable time, will be abolished in order that the ruler may have time for control and consideration. His power will not then be split up into fractional parts among time-serving favourites who surround the throne for its pomp and splendour, and are interested only in their own and not in the common interests of the State.

Economic crises have been produced by us from the *goyim* by no other means than the withdrawal of money from circulation. Huge capitals have stagnated, withdrawing money from States, which were constantly obliged to apply to those same stagnant capitals for loans. These loans burdened the finances of the State with the payment of interest and made them the bond slaves of these capitals.... The concentration of industry in the hands of capitalists out of the hands of small masters has drained away all the juices of the peoples and with them also of the States....

The present issue of money in general does not correspond with the requirements per head, and cannot therefore satisfy all the needs of the workers. The issue of money ought to correspond with the growth of population and thereby children also must absolutely be reckoned as consumers of currency from the day of their birth. The revision of issue is a material question for the whole world.

You are aware that the gold standard has been the ruin of the States which adopted it, for it has not been able to satisfy the demands for money, the more so that we have removed gold from circulation as far as possible.

With us the standard that must be introduced is the cost of working-man power, whether it be reckoned in paper or in wood. We shall make the issue of money in accordance with the normal requirements of each subject, adding to the quantity with every birth and subtracting with every death.

The accounts will be managed by each department (the French administrative division), each circle.

In order that there may be no delays in paying out of money for State needs the sums and terms of such payments will be fixed by decree of the ruler; this will do away with the protection by a ministry of one institution to the detriment of others.

The budgets of income and expenditure will be carried out side by side that they may not be obscured by distance one to another.

The reforms projected by us in the financial institutions and principles of the *goyim* will be clothed by us in such forms as will alarm nobody. We shall point out the necessity of reforms in consequence of the disorderly darkness into which the *goyim* by their irregularities have plunged the finances. The first irregularity, as we shall point out, consists in their beginning with drawing up a single budget which year after year grows owing to the following cause: this budget is dragged out to half the year, then they demand a budget to put things right, and this they expend in three months, after which they ask for a supplementary budget, and all this ends with a liquidation budget. But, as the budget of the following year is drawn up in accordance with the sum of the total addition, the annual departure from the normal reaches as much as 50 percent in a year, and so the annual budget is trebled in ten years. Thanks to such methods, allowed by the carelessness of the goy States, their treasuries are empty. The period of loans supervenes, and that has swallowed up remainders and brought all the goy States to bankruptcy.

You understand perfectly that economic arrangements of this kind, which have been suggested to the *goyim* by us, cannot be carried on by us.

Every kind of loan proves infirmity in the State and a want of understanding of the rights of the State. Loans hang like a sword of Damocles over the heads of rulers, who, instead of taking from their subjects by a temporary tax, come begging with oustretched palm of our bankers. Foreign loans are leeches which there is no possibility of removing from the body of the State until they fall off of themselves or the State flings them off. But the goy States do not tear them off; they go on in persisting in putting more on to themselves so that they must inevitably perish, drained by voluntary blood-letting.

What also indeed is, in substance, a loan, especially a foreign loan? A loan is — an issue of government bills of exchange containing a percentage obligation commensurate to the sum of the loan capital. If the loan bears a charge of 5 per cent, then in twenty years the State vainly pays away in interest a sum equal to the loan borrowed, in forty years it is paying a double sum, in sixty — treble, and all the while the debt remains an unpaid debt.

From this calculation it is obvious that with any form of taxation per head the State is baling out the last coppers of the poor taxpayers in order to settle accounts with wealthy foreigners, from whom it has borrowed money instead of collecting these coppers for its own needs without the additional interest.

So long as loans were internal the *goyim* only shuffled money from the pockets of the poor to those of the rich, but when we bought up the necessary person in order to transfer loans into the external sphere all the wealth of States flowed into our cash-boxes and all the *goyim* began to pay us the tribute of subjects.

If the superficiality of goy kings on their thrones in regard to State affairs and the venality of ministers or the want of understanding of financial matters on the part of other ruling persons have made their countries debtors to our treasuries to amounts quite impossible to pay it has not been accomplished without on our part heavy expenditure of trouble and money.

Stagnation of money will not be allowed by us and therefore there will be no State-interest bearing paper, except a one-percent series, so that there will be no payment of interest to leeches that suck all the strength out of the State. The right to issue interest-bearing paper will be given exclusively to industrial companies who will find no difficulty in paying interest out of profits, whereas the State does not make interest on borrowed money like these companies, for the State borrows to spend and not to use in operations.

Industrial papers will be bought also by the government which from being as now a payer of tribute by loan operations will be transformed into a lender of money at a profit. This measure will stop the stagnation of money, parasitic profits and idleness, all of which were useful for us among the *goyim* so long as they were independent but are not desirable under our rule.

How clear is the undeveloped power of thought of the purely brute brains of the *goyim*, as expressed in the fact that they have been borrowing from us with payment of interest without ever thinking that all the same these very moneys plus an addition for payment of interest must be got by them from their own State pockets in order to settle up with us. What could have been simpler than to take the money they wanted from their own people?

But it is a proof of the genius of our chosen mind that we have contrived to present the matter of loans to them in such a light that they have even seen in them an advantage for themselves.

Our accounts, which we shall present when the time comes, in the light of centuries of experience gained by experiments made by us on the goy States, will be distinguished by clearness and definiteness and will show at a glance to all men the advantage of our innovations. They will put an end to those abuses to which we owe our mastery over the *goyim*, but which cannot be allowed in our kingdom.

We shall so hedge about our system of accounting that neither the ruler nor the most insignificant public servant will be in a position to divert even the smallest sum from its destination without detection or to direct it in another direction except that which will be once fixed in a definite plan of action.

And without a definite plan it is impossible to rule. Marching along an undetermined road and with undetermined resources brings to ruin by the way heroes and demi-gods.

The goy rulers, whom we once upon a time advised should be distracted from State occupations by representatives receptions, observances of etiquette, entertainments, were only screens for our rule. The accounts of favourite courtiers who replaced them in the sphere of affairs were drawn up for them by our agents, and every time gave satisfaction to short-sighted minds by promises that in the future economies and improvements were foreseen.... Economies from what? From new taxes? — were questions that might have been but were not asked by those who read our accounts and projects....

You know to what they have been brought by this carelessness, to what a pitch of financial disorder they have arrived, notwithstanding the astonishing industry of their peoples. . .

PROTOCOL NO. 21

Internal loans. Debit and taxes. Conversions. Bankruptcy. Savings banks and rentes. Abolition of money markets. Regulation of industrial values.

To what I reported to you at the last meeting I shall now add a detailed explanation of internal loans. Of foreign loans I shall say nothing more, because they have fed us with the national moneys of the *goyim*, but for our State there will be no foreigners, that is, nothing external.

We have taken advantage of the venality of administrators and the slackness of rulers to get our moneys twice, thrice and more times over, by lending to the goy governments moneys which were not at all needed by the States. Could anyone do the like in regard to us?...Therefore, I shall only deal with the details of internal loans.

States announce that such a loan is to be concluded and open subscriptions for their own bills of exchange, that is, for their interest-bearing paper. That they may be within the reach of all the price is determined at from a hundred to a thousand; and a discount is made for the earliest subscribers. Next day by artificial means the price of them goes up, the alleged reason being that everyone is rushing to buy them. In a few days the treasury safes are as they say overflowing and there's more money than they can do with (why then take it?). The subscription, it is alleged, covers many times over the issue total of the loan: in this lies the whole stage effect — look you, they say, what confidence is shown in the government's bills of exchange.

But when the comedy is played out there emerges the fact that a debit and an exceedingly burdensome debit has been created. For the payment of interest it becomes necessary to have recource to new loans, which do not swallow up but only add to the capital debt. And when this credit is exhausted it becomes necessary by new taxes to cover, not the loan, but only the interest on it. These taxes are a debit employed to cover a debit.

Later comes the time for conversions, but they diminish the payment of interest without covering the debt, and besides they cannot be made without the consent of the lenders; on announcing a conversion a proposal is made to return the money to those who are not willing to convert their paper. If everybody expressed his unwillingness and demanded his money back, the government would be hooked on their own flies and would be found insolvent and unable to pay the proposed sums. By good luck the subjects of the goy governments, knowing nothing about financial affairs, have always preferred losses on exchange and diminution of interest to the risk of new investments of their moneys, and have thereby many a time enabled these governments to throw off their shoulders a debit of several millions.

Nowadays, with external loans, these tricks cannot be played by the *goyim* for they know that we shall demand all our moneys back.

In this way an acknowledged bankruptcy will best prove to the various countries the absence of any means between the interests of the peoples and of those who rule them.

I beg you to concentrate your particular attention upon this point, and upon the following: nowadays all internal loans are consolidated by so-called flying loans, that is, such as have terms of payment more or less near. These debts consist of moneys paid into the savings banks and reserve funds. It left for long at the disposition of a government these funds evaporate in the payment of interest on foreign loans, and are replaced by the deposit of equivalent amount of *rentes.*

And these last it is which patch up all the leaks in the State treasuries of the *goyim*.

When we ascend the throne of the world all these financial and similar shifts, as being not in accord with our interests, will be swept away so as not to leave a trace, as also will be destroyed all money markets, since we shall not allow the prestige of our power to be shaken by fluctuations of prices set upon our values, which we shall announce by law at the price which represents their full worth without any possibility of lowering or raising (Raising gives the pretext for lowering, which indeed was where we made a beginning in relation to the values of the *goyim*.)

We shall replace the money markets by grandiose government credit institutions, the object of which will be to fix the price of industrial values in accordance with government views. These institutions will be in a position to fling upon the market five hundred millions of industrial paper in one day, or to buy up for the same amount. In this way all industrial undertakings will come into dependence upon us. You may imagine for yourselves what immense power we shall thereby secure for ourselves....

PROTOCOL NO. 22

The secret of what is coming. The evil of many centuries as the foundation of future well-being. The aureole of power and its mystical worship.

In all that has so far been reported by me to you, I have endeavoured to depict with care the secret of what is coming, of what is past, and of what is going on now, rushing into the flood of the great events coming already in the near future, the secret of our relations to the *goyim* and of financial operations. On this subject there remains still a little for me to add.

In our hands is the greatest power of our day — gold: in two days we can procure from our storehouses any quantity we may please.

Surely there is no need to seek further proof that our rule is predestined by God? Surely we shall not fail with such wealth to prove that all that evil which for so many centuries we have had to commit has served at the end of ends the cause of true well-being — the bringing of everything into order? Though it be even by the exercise of some violence, yet all the same it will be established. We shall contrive to prove that we are benefactors who have restored to the rend and mangled earth the true good and also freedom of the person, and therewith we shall enable it to be enjoyed in peace and quiet, with proper dignity of relations, on the condition, of course, of strict observance of the laws established by us. We shall make plain therewith that freedom does not consist in dissipation and in the right of unbridled licence any more than the dignity and force of a man do not consist in the right for everyone to promulgate destructive principles in the nature of freedom of conscience, equality and the like, that freedom of the person in no wise consists in the right to agitate oneself and others by abominable speeches before disorderly mobs, and that true freedom consists in the inviolability of the person who honourably and strictly observes all the laws of life in common, that human dignity is wrapped up in consciousness of the rights and also of the absence of rights of each, and not wholly and solely in fantastic imaginings about the subject of one's ego.

Our authority will be glorious because it will be all powerful, will rule and guide, and not muddle along after leaders and orators shrieking themselves hoarse with senseless words which they call great principles and which are nothing else, to speak honestly, but utopian....Our authority will be the crown of order, and in that is included the whole happiness of man. The aureole of this authority will inspire a mystical bowing of the knee before it and a reverent fear before it of all the peoples. True force makes no terms with any right, not even with that of God; none dare come near to it so as to take so much as a span from it away.

PROTOCOL NO. 23

Reduction of the manufacture of articles of luxury. Small master production. Unemployment. Prohibition of drunkenness. Killing out of the old society and its resurrection in a new form. The chosen one of God.

That the peoples may become accustomed to obedience it is necessary to inculcate lessons of humility and therefore to reduce the production of articles of luxury. By this we shall improve morals which have been debased by emulation in the sphere of luxury. We shall re-establish small master production which will mean laying a mine under the private capital of manufacturers. This is indispensable also for the reason that manufacturers on the grand scale often move, though not always consciously, the thoughts of the masses in directions against the government. A people of small masters knows nothing of unemployment and this binds him closely with existing order, and consequently with the firmness of authority. Unemployment is a most perilous thing for a government. For us its part will have been played out the moment authority is transferred into our hands. Drunkenness also will be prohibited by law and punishable as a crime against the humanness of man who is turned into a brute under the influence of alcohol.

Subjects, I repeat once more, give blind obedience only to the strong hand which is absolutely independent of them, for in it they feel the sword for defense and support against social scourges.... What do they want with an angelic spirit in a king? What they have to see in him is the personification of force and power.

The supreme lord who will replace all now existing rulers, dragging on their existence among societies demoralized by us, societies that have denied even the authority of God, from whose midst breaks out on all sides the fire of anarchy, must first of all proceed to quench this all-devouring flame. Therefore he will be obliged to kill off those existing societies, though he should drench them with his own blood, that he may resurrect them again in the form of regularly organized troops fighting consciously with every kind of infection that may cover the body of the State with sores.

This Chosen One of God is chosen from above to demolish the senseless forces moved by instinct and not reason, by brutishness and not humanness. These forces now triumph in manifestations of robbery and every kind of violence under the mask of principles of freedom and rights. They have overthrown all forms of social order to erect on the ruins the throne of the King of the Jews; but their part will be played out the moment he enters into his kingdom. Then it will be necessary to sweep them away from his path, on which must be left no knot, no splinter.

Then will it be possible for us to say to the peoples of the world: "Give thanks to God and bow the knee before him who bears on his front the seal of the predestination of man, to which God himself has led his star that none other but Him might free us from all the before-mentioned forces and evils."

PROTOCOL NO. 24

Confirming the roots of King David (?). Training of the king. Setting aside of direct heirs. The king and three of his sponsors. The king is fate. Irreproachability of exterior morality of the King of the Jews.

I pass now to the method of confirming the dynastic roots of King David to the last strata of the earth.

This confirmation will first and foremost be included in that in which to this day has rested the force of conservatism by our learned elders of the conduct of all the affairs of the world, in the directing of the education of thought of all humanity.

Certain members of the seed of David will prepare the kings and their heirs, selecting not by right of heritage but by eminent capacities, inducting them into the most secret mysteries of the political, into schemes of government, but providing always that none may come to knowledge of the secrets. The object of this mode of action is that all may know that government cannot be entrusted to those who have not been inducted into the secret places of its art....

To these persons only will be taught the practical application of the aforenamed plans by comparison of the experiences of many centuries, all the observations on the politico-economic moves and social sciences — in a word, all the spirit of laws which have been unshakably established by nature herself for the regulation of the relations of humanity.

Direct heirs will often be set aside from ascending the throne if in their time of training they exhibit frivolity, softness and other qualities that are the ruin of authority, which render them incapable of governing and in themselves dangerous for kingly office.

Only those who are unconditionally capable for firm, even if it be to cruelty, direct rule will receive the reins of rule from our learned elders.

In case of falling sick with weakness of will or other form of incapacity, kings must by law hand over the reins of rule to new and capable hands.

The king's plans of action for the current moment, and all the more so for the future, will be unknown, even to those who are called his closest counsellors.

Only the king and the three who stood sponsor for him will know what is coming.

In the person of the king who with unbending will is master of himself and of humanity all will discern as it were fate with its mysterious ways. None will know what the king wishes to attain by his dispositions, and therefore none will dare to stand across an unknown path.

It is understood that the brain reservoir of the king must correspond in capacity to the plan of government it has to contain. It is for this reason that he will ascend the throne not otherwise than after examination of his mind by the aforesaid learned elders.

That the people may know and love their king it is indispensable for him to converse in the market-places with his people. This ensures the necessary clinching of the two forces which are now divided one from another by us by the terror.

This terror was indispensable for us till the time come; for both these forces separately to fall under our influence.

The King of the Jews must not be at the mercy of his passions, and especially of sensuality: on no side of his character must he give brute instinct power over his mind. Sensuality worse than all else disorganizes the capacities of the mind and clearness of views, distracting the thoughts to the worst and most brutal side of human activity.

The prop of humanity in the person of the supreme lord of all the world of the holy seed of David must sacrifice to his people all personal inclinations.

Our supreme lord must be of an exemplary irreproachability.

LORD SYDENHAM ON THE 'PROTOCOLS'

The following letter appeared in the "Spectator" of August 27th, 1921, and the late Lord Sydenham kindly consented to its reproduction.]

Sir—When the Protocols first appeared in English it was pointed out that they embodied a forgery perpetrated by the Tsar's police with the idea of promoting pogroms. It now appears that they are adapted from a "pamphlet" of 1865 attacking the Second Empire." This is most interesting, but it explains nothing. As you point out, Mrs. Webster has shown the Protocols to be full of plagiarism which she effectively explained by the use of parallel columns, and before her most able book appeared Mr. Lucien Wolfe had traced other similarities. As the Protocols were obviously a compilation this was to be expected, and further resemblances may be discovered. The importance of the most sinister compilation that has ever appeared resides in the subject matter. The Protocols explain in almost laborious detail the objects of Bolshevism and the methods of carrying it into effect. These methods were in operation in 1901 when Nilus said that he received the documents, but Bolshevism was then Marxian Communism, and the time had not come for applying it by military force. Nothing that was written in 1865 can have any bearing upon the deadly accuracy of the forecasts in the Protocol, most of which have since been fulfilled to the letter. Moreover, the principles they enunciate corresponds closely with the recorded statements of Jewish authorities. If you read the American edition, with its valuable annexes, you will understand this, and the confirmatory quotations there given can be multiplied. Even the "Jewish World Despotism," which you described as a "piece of malignant lunacy," is not obscurely hinted at. Take this one quotation from Jewish State, by Theodore Herzl: "Where we sink we become revolutionary proletariat, the subordinate officers of the revolutionary party: when we rise, there rises also our terrible power of the purse." Compare this ominous statement with those of the Protocols, of which it is plainly an echo.

I note with thankfulness that you say that the discovery of the French pamphlet "does not clear up the whole mystery." Indeed it does not, and if you will carefully read Mr. Ford's amazing disclosure you will wish for more light. The main point is, of course, the source from which Nilus obtained the Protocols. The Russians who knew Nilus and his writings cannot all have been exterminated by the Bolsheviks. His book, in which the Protocols only form one chapter, has not been translated though it would give some idea of the man. He was, I have been told by a Russian lady, absolutely incapable either of writing any portion of the Protocols or of being a party to fraud.

What is the most striking characteristic of the Protocols? The answer is knowledge of a rare kind, embracing the widest field. The solution of the "Mystery," if it is one, is to be found by ascertaining where this uncanny knowledge on which prophecies now literally fulfilled are based, can be shown to reside.—I am, Sir, &c.,

SYDENHAM

ADDENDUM

STARTLING NEW DOCUMENTS

The manifesto of Aldolphe Cremieux, addressed to the National Jewry on the occasion of the founding of the Universal Israelite Alliance. This has been pronounced a forgery, and something much less produce as the "real" thing. The unfortunate part of the business is that the "forgery" corresponds infinitely more closely with the *facts* of history that that which is claimed to be genuine! It proclaims three incontrovertible truths: (1) That the Jewish Nation is the enemy of all nations; (2) That Jews claim that they are a people "Chosen" to dominate the whole earth, and take possession of all the riches of all peoples; (3) That the power of all nations is already in their hands, and that Jews thing they are on the eve of their complete conquest of the rest of the human race. The date of this Protocol II, of our series, is 1860.

A PROTOCOL OF 1860

We take this PROTOCOL from the ***Morning Post*** of September 6th, 1920:

A correspondent writing in reference to the hidden perils draws attention to a Manifesto issued in 1880 to the 'Jews of the Universe.' by Adolphe Cremieux, the founder of the Allience Israelite Universelle, and the well-known member of the Provisional Government of 1871. Adolphe Cremieux, while Grand Master of the French Masonic Lodges, offered 1,000,000 franks for the head of William I of Germany. On his tomb he requested the following sole inscription to be inscribed:

"'Here lies Adolphe Cremieux, the founder of the *Alliance Israelite Universelle.*'"

THE MANIFESTO

Emblem: On top - the tablets of Moses, a little lower - tow extended hands clasping each other, and as a basis of the whole - the glove of the earth.

Motto: "All Jews for one, and one for all."

The union which we desire to found will not be a French, English, Irish, or German union, but a Jewish one, a Universal one.

Other peoples and races are divided into nationalities; we alone have not co-citizens, but exclusively co-religionaries.

A Jew will under no circumstances become the friend of a Christian or a Moslem before the moment arrives when the light of the Jewish Faith, the only religion of reason, will shine all over the world.

Scattered amongst other nations, who from time immemorial were hostile to our rights and interests, we desire primarily to be and to remain immutably Jews.

Our nationality is the religion of our fathers, and we recognize no other nationality.

We are living in foreign lands, and cannot trouble about the mutable ambitions of countries entirely alien to us, while our own moral and material problems are endangered.

The Jewish teaching must cover the whole earth. Israelites! No matter where fate should lead - though scattered all over the earth, you must always consider yourselves members of a Chosen Race.

If you realize that the Faith of your forefathers is your only patriotism—

—If you recognize that, notwithstanding the nationalities you have embrace, you always remain and everywhere form one and only nation—

—If you believe that JEWRY only is the one and only religious and political truth—

—If you are convinced of this, you, Israelites of the Universe—

—Then come and give ear to our appeal and prove to us your consent!...

Our cause is great and holy, and its success is guaranteed. Catholicism, our immemorial enemy, is lying in the dust, mortally wounded in the head.

The net which Israel is throwing over the globe of the earth is widening and spreading daily, and the momentous prophecies of our holy books are at last to be realized.

The time is near when Jerusalem will become the house of payer for all nations and peoples, and the banner of Jewish Mono-deity will be unfurled and hoisted on the most distant shores.

Let us avail ourselves of all circumstances.

Our might is immense - learn to adopt this for our cause. What have you to be afraid of?

The day is not distant when all the riches and treasures of the earth will become the property of the Children of Israel."

More than sixty years have elapsed since this Protocol was written, and the riches of the earth are now almost entirely in the posses or under the control of the Children of Israel. The Torah, said the Jew poet, Heine, is the Jews' "portable Fatherland." Cremieux says practically the same thing—"the faith of our fathers is your only patriotism." The Jew regards all Non Jews as foreigners, and he is an alien everywhere.

FUNERAL ORATION (1923)

THE FATAL DISCOURSE OF RABBI REICHHORN

Appended to the prophecies of this Protocol we have put a few of the events which have happened in fulfillment. It will be seen that there is a close correspondence between this Protocol, the Cremieux Manifesto, and the epistle emanating from the "Prince of the Jews" in 1489 A.D., and published in a Rothschild magazine. It is probable that when any Gentile would ever think of connecting it with other documents emanating from Jewry, or with modern happenings.

In its issue of 21 October, 1920, (no. 195) *La Vieille France* published an extremely important Russian document in which the following passage occurs:

"There is a striking analogy between the *Protocols of the Elders of Zion* and the discourse of the Rabbi Reichhorn, pronounce in Prague in…over the tomb of the Grand Rabbi Simeon-ben-Ihuda and published by Readcliffe, *who paid with his life for the divulgation:* Sonol, who had taken Radcliffe to hear Reichhorn was killed in a duel some time afterwards. The general ideas formulated by the Rabbi are fully developed in the Protocols."

In its issue of 10 March 1921 (No. 214) La Vieille France gives the version of this funeral oration which was published in *La Russie Juive*. It is perfectly clear that the funeral oration and the Protocols of the Elders of Zion come from one and the same mint. Both are prophetic; and the power which made the prophecies has been able to bring about their fulfillment. This oration is so important that we append to it an account of the fulfillment of each of the sections. There can no longer be any doubts as to whose is the power which is disturbing the world, creating World Unrest, and at the same time reaping all the profits. Jewry is Enslaving all Christian people of the Earth. There IS a Jew World Plot and it now stands finally and completely unmasked.

1. *Every hundred years, We, the Sages of Israel,* have been accustomed to meet in Sanhedrin in order to examine our progress toward the Domination

of the World which Jehovah has promised us, [actually it was Satan who promised all the kingdoms of the world to Christ if he would worship him], and our conquest over the enemy - Christianity.

2. This year, united over the tomb of our reverend **Simeon-ben-Ihuda**, we can state with pride that the past century has brought us very near to our goal, and that this goal will be very soon attained.

3. *Gold has always* been and always will be the irresistible power. Handled by expert hands it will always be the most useful lever for those who possess it, and the object of envy for those who do not. With gold we can buy the most rebellious conscience, can fix the rate of all values, the current price of all products, can subsidize all State loans, and thereafter hold the states at our mercy.

4. Already the principal banks, the exchanges of the entire world, the credits of all governments, are in our hands.

5. The other great power of The Press. By repeating without cessation certain ideas, the Press succeeds in the end in having them accepted as actualities. The Theater renders us analogous services. Everywhere the Press and the Theater obey our orders.

6. By the ceaseless praise of *Democratic Rule* we shall divide the Christians into political parties, we shall destroy the unity of their nations, we shall sow discord everywhere. Reduced to impotence, they will bow before the *Law of Our Bank, always* united, and always devoted to our Cause.

7. We shall Force the Christians into Wars by exploiting their pride and their stupidity. They will massacre each other, and clear the ground for us to put our own people into.

8. The possession of the land has always brought influence and power. In the name of social Justice and Equality we shall parcel out the great estates; we shall give the fragments to the peasants who covet them with all their powers, and who will soon be in debt to us by the expense of cultivating them. Our capital will make us their masters. We in our turn shall become the great proprietors, and the possession of the land will assure the power to us.

9. Let us try replace the circulation of gold with paper money; our chests will absorb the gold, and we shall regulate the value of the paper which will make us masters of all the positions.

10. We count among us plenty of orators capable of feigning enthusiasm and of persuading mobs. We shall spread them among the people to announce changes which should secure the happiness of the human race. By gold and by flattery we shall gain the proletariat which will charge itself with annihilating *Christian* Capitalism. We shall promise workmen salaries of which they have never dared to dream, but we shall also raise the price of necessities so that *our profits will be greater still.*

11. In this manner we shall prepare Revolutions which the *Christians will make themselves* and of which we shall reap the fruit.

12. By our mockeries and our attacks upon them we shall make their Priest and Preachers ridiculous then odious, and their religion as ridiculous and as odious as their Clergy. Then we shall be masters of their sculs. For our pious attachment to our own religion and the superiority of our souls.

13. We shall already established our own men in all important positions. We must endeavor to provide the Goyim with lawyers and doctors; the lawyers are au courant with all interests; doctors once in the house, become confessors and directors of consciences.

14. But above all let us monopolize education. By this means: *we spread ideas that are useful to us,* and shape the children's brains as suits us.

15. If one of our people should unhappily fall into the hands of justice amongst the Christians, we must rush to help him; find as many witnesses as he needs to save him from his judges, until we become judges ourselves.

16. The monarchs of the Christian world, swollen with ambition and vanity, surround themselves with luxury and with numerous armies. *We shall furnish them with all the money their folly demands,* and so shall keep them in leash.

17. Let us take care not to hinder the marriage of our men with christian girls, for through them we shall get out foot into the most closely locked circles. If our daughter marry Goyim they will be no less useful, *for the children of a JEWISH mother are ours.* Let us foster the idea of free love that we may destroy among Christian women attachment to the principles and practices of their religion.

18. For ages past the sons of Israel, despised and persecuted have been working to open up a path to power. They are hitting the mark. *they control the economic life of the accursed christians*; their influence preponderates over politics and over manners.

19. At the wished for hour, fixed in advance, *we shall let loose the revolution,* which by ruining all classes of christianity will *definitely enslave the christians* to us. Thus will be accomplished the promise of God made to His People.

THE FULFILLMENT OF THE PROPHECIES (1923)

[The "God" who promised to give all the kingdoms of the world and the glory of them" to his worshiper we know. He is the God of Judas, of Herod and of Cain. Let us now see how he has carried out his promise. Paragraph by paragraph we will take the items. Let our readers compare them by their numbers.]

1. Within the half century which has elapsed since this prophetic oration was made, Judaism has taken giant strides in its conquests over its age-long "Enemy" - Christianity. Purses, Press, Politics - these are the engines by means of which the Elders of Zion have made their conquest.

2. Four of the Christian Empires - Russia, Austria, Germany and France - have already succumbed to the Jew Power. Only the British Empire is left, and all its most precious institutions are already under Jew control, which is working ceaselessly for its final betrayal.

3. The *Gold* of the Nations is the real *Lord of Israel.* The Gold mart of England is close on the Jews' "Holy days!" Said the Evening Standard, October 12, 1921.—*"Gold was unregistered today owning to the Jewish religious observance."* In the Jews' expert hands gold has brought Parliament, Premiers, Parties, Principles and Consciences, as the doings of the Parliament which was one England's reveal. Jews have flooded all nations with paper money, retaining the gold themselves. They control all the exchanges of the world and fix or unfix the rates of exchanges as suits their interests. Jews have raised prices pari passu with wages and so have kept up Industrial Unrest, which is one of their chief assets.

4. As for principal Banks and Exchanges, the names of Rothschild, Gwinner, Speyer, Schiff, Lowb, Kahn, Kuhn, Casssel, Samuel, Warburg, Guggenheim, sufficiently attest the Overlordship of Jewry in Lucre's Empire.

5. But without control of the World's Press, the power of Gold could not be maintained. The Press of the one country would not be sufficient. Hence the necessity of securing control of all lines of communication, press agencies, Wolff Bureaux, Reuter's, Agence Hava, Marconi's, advertisement agencies as well as the actual ownership of papers, such as exists throughout the world today. In our own country there is not a single daily morning paper, except the Morning Post, which has any freedom form Jew control. The theaters and cinemas are equally tied, and the British Public are treated to Jew propaganda plays like the "Little Brother,", "Welcome Stranger," "The Wandering Jew," and Mr. Levy's lavatory-and-bead-chamber plays in his Grand Guignol. "Everywhere the press and the Theatre *are under our orders.*" And the Jews are so well place in regard to cinemas that they boast that they cans *censor their own* films! *(Jewish Guardian).*

6. "Liberalism" is one of the chief instruments of the Jewish power. Through preaching this doctrine, and getting into the machinery of Liberal parties Jews have exploited for their own ends the generous instincts of all the peoples who have received them into their communities. Jews have preached "democracy," and through getting their dupes to believe in it, have succeeded in riveting on their necks the chain of Shylocracy, the rule of the Crowned Usurer. Shylock-Rothschild, who was admitted to England's parliament by "Liberal" statement, now rules the world. Reduced to impotence the Nations

bow before the Law - not of Moses even, but of the Jew's Bank - "always united and always devoted to our (Jewish) cause."

7. Thanks to the terrible power of this Bank, Jews have forced Christians into wars without numbers, culminating in the Great War. Wars have this especial value for Jews that Christians massacre each other and make more room for the Chosen People. Moreover, as Werner Sombart truly says, *"Wars are the Jews Harvest." The Jews' Bank* grows fat on the wars of Christians. Nearly one hundred millions of Christians have been sweep off the face of the globe already by the War, which the Jews planned, and which is not yet by any means over in spite of official "Peace" celebrations, and the Lords of Gold are stronger than ever.

8. By Jew-made laws the ancient proprietors of England are being rapidly deprive of their estates, and farmers and laborers are at the same time becoming more and more completely enslaved under Shylock's power.

9. Jews have the gold and we have paper money. Jews give the paper the "value" which suits their interest. So that a good harvest may mean ruin to a farmer just as readily as a bad one through Jew manipulation of prices and exchanges. At the present day, for purposes of selling, a litter of pedigree puppies will fetch as much as a good-sized stack of hay, although the hay well feed just as many horses ad it did when hay was five times its present price.

10. Oratory is another great asset of the Gold-Power of Jewry. Shinwells in Scotland, Monds in Wales, De Valeras in Ireland, Isaacses and Samuels in England and India with their Gentile Front megaphones like Lloyd George, Asquith, Churchill, McKenna, MacDonald, Henderson, Lansbury, Tom Mann, Watson, etc., are all serving the Jew's end. By gold and false promises they turn the proletariat *against Christian capitalists* - who are often not capitalists at all but actual producers - and divert their attentions from the real Shylocks who are the actual villains of the piece. By raising the workman's wages to an impossible live they destroy trade, and by raising the prices of food they produce at once Unemployment and Starvation which make the enslaving power of Shylock and his tribe greater than ever.

11. Thus come *Revolution* in which Christians do all the fighting and of which Jews reap all the profits. Russia is completely destroyed by the Jews. Revolution has broken out in the Empire of Britain. Ireland is almost a Republic, in fact, if not in name, and the Jews are prospering amazingly. Our so-called "British" Cabinet is in point of fact a Bolshevik Cabinet in preliminary stage.

12. Thanks to Jew educationalists in the Press and on the platform, the Churches are suffering from creeping paralysis. The Jews are preaching atheism to Christians, that Judaism may remain alone in the field. Mond with his *English Review* was doing the educational work of his tribe in polluting the minds of English readers.

13. The power of Jewry has put its own sons or its own Gentile agents in all positions of strategic importance. We have seen the Lloyed George-Sassoon combination presiding over the empire; Isaacs, Samuel Meyer over India; Samuel over Palestine; Mond over the health of the Kingdom; to name only a few samples in this country, and in other countries it is even worse; whilst the League of Nations - as the Jews themselves boast - is essentially a Jewish concern.

14. As for the monopoly of education, the names Magnuses, Gollanczec, Waldsteins, Lees, Lowes, Hatogs, Monds, etc., etc., show how rotten with Judaism are the educational establishments of this country. The Professorial Chairs of Germany and France are almost all filled with Jews.

15. Jews are so fond of "Law" that they are rapidly monopolizing it. This helps them in many ways. How Jews defeat justice is shown by the Dreyfus case, and by the case of the Jews who murdered Pere Thomas, the Roman Catholic Priest of Damascus, and his servant. The murder was a ritual murder, but thanks to the efforts of the Jewish nation, headed by Adolphe Cremieux of France and Moses Montefiore of England the murderers, although tried and convicted on the clearest evidence, escaped the penalty.

16. The crowned monarchs of the world are led by the Jews, as the German Emperor was by Walther Rathenau before and during the war. Jews lend monarchs money in order that they may work with it their own destruction. Jews can manipulate republics more easily than they can monarchies and that is one reason why they foster revolutions.

17. The intermarriage of wealthy sons and daughter of Jews into aristocratic families has polluted almost all the once noble houses of the Christian world. Not to mention Jew "Peers," there are the examples of Lord Rosebery and the Rothschilds, and number of Jew duchesses. Lord Crewe is married to the daughter of a Rothschild, and Lord Derby married his daughter to Lord Dalmeny, a Rothschild's son; Lord Sheffield married his daughter to the Jew Edwin Samuel alias Montagu. Lord Curzon of Kedlestone is son-in-law of a Jew.

18. After "Society," Commerce. "Lyons" control the catering trade of the metropolis; Samuel controls petrol; Mond controls nickel and chemicals; Salmon and Gluckstein and their co-tribesmen control tobacco, etc., etc. and so the "accrued Christians" tamely submit to the yoke of Israel.

19. The British Empire, so far as concerns its own coin (which the Jews control) is bankrupt. But its real wealth is greater than ever - its spirit, its courage, its ancient literature before Jewry touch it with polluting fingers, its enterprise, its deep down desire to fulfill its mission in the world - this is England's real wealth, and this wealth Jewry hopes to annihilate by means of Revolution and by planting England's crown family on Shylock's head.

20. England's hour has not struck yet. May the sleeping giant awake in time to burst the paper bonds which England's indolence and England's generosity have combine to suffer Shylock to wind round England's limbs!

A PROTOCOL OF 1919

A Russian newspaper, *Prizyv,* of 5th February, 1920, published in Berlin, contained an interesting document in *Hebrew,* dated December, 1919, which was found in the pocket of the dead Jew Zunder, the Bolshevik Commander of the 11th Sharp-shooter Battalion, throwing light on the secret organizations of Jewry in Russia.

This Protocol has, like the first, never been called in question by the Nation of Jewry. It reveals identically the same plans and purposed of the Jews for World domination and revenge which pervade them all. This one especially gloats over the Jew conquest and enslavement of Russia.

In extenso it ran as follows:

SECRET—To the representatives of all the branches of the Israelite International League.

Sons of Israel! The hour of our ultimate victory is near. We stand on the threshold to the command of the world. That, which we could only dream of before us is about to be realized. Only quite recently feeble and powerless, we can now, thanks to the world's catastrophe, raise our heads with pride.

We must, however, be careful. It can surely be prophesied that, after we have marched over ruined and broken altars and thrones, we shall advance further on the same indicated path.

The authority of the, to us, alien religions and doctrines of faith we have, through very successful propaganda, subjected to a merciless criticism and mockery. We have brought the culture, civilization, traditions and thrones of the Christian nations to stagger. We have done everything to bring the Russian people under the yoke of the Jewish power, and ultimately compelled them to fall on their knees before us.

We have nearly completed all this but we must all the same be very cautious, because the oppressed Russia is our arch-enemy. The victory over Russia, gained through our intellectual superiority, may in future, in a new generation turn against us.

Russia is conquered and brought to the ground. Russia is in the agony of death under our heel, but do not forget — not even for a moment — that we must be careful! The holy care for our safety does not allow us to show either pity or mercy. At last we have been allowed to behold the bitter need of the Russian people, and to see it in tears! By taking from them their property, their gold, we have reduced this people to helpless slaves.

Be cautious and silent! *We ought to have no mercy for our enemy. We must make an end of the best and leading elements* of the Russian people, so that the vanquished Russia may not find any leader! Thereby every possibility will vanquish for them to resist our power. *We must excite hatred and disputes between workers and peasants.* War and class-struggle will destroy all treasures and culture created by the Christian people. But be cautious, Sons of Israel! Our victory is near, because our *political and economic power and influence* upon the masses are in rapid progress. We buy up Government loans and gold, and thereby we have controlling power over the world's exchanges. The power is in our hands, but be careful — place no faith in traitorous shady powers!

Bronstein (Trotsky), Apfelbaum (Zinovieff), Rosenfeld (Kameneff), Steinberg — all of them are like unto thousands of other true sons of Israel. Our power in Russia is unlimited. In the towns, the Commissariats and Commissions of Food, House Commissions, etc., are dominated by our people. But do not let victory intoxicate you. Be careful, cautious, because no one except yourselves will protect us!

Remember we cannot rely on the Red Army, which one day may turn its warfare on ourselves.

Sons of Israel! The hour for our long-cherished victory over Russia is near; close up solid your ranks! Make known our people's national policy! Fight for eternal ideals! Keep holy the old laws, which history has bequeathed to us!

Signed, The Central Committee of the Petersburg Branch of the Israelite International League.

It will be noted that the above was found in *Hebrew,* as the original at the Protocols of the Elders of Zion and all the secret documents of the Jew are. There are plenty of manifestoes i Christian languages that are intended for the Goyim to read. Of these we need take no account. "Israelite International League" can be none other than *l'Alliance Israelite Universelle,* found by Cremieux and headed by Rothschild.

All the Protocols tell the same tale of malice, revenge, cupidity and murderous hate against Christians and Christianity. Judaism is Satanism; and no amount of ritual and Kabalistic camouflage can hide this fact.